PROTECT YOUR HOME

A Common-Sense Guide to Home Security

by
Richard H. Geiger

A Garden Way Publishing Book

STOREY

Storey Communications, Inc.
Schoolhouse Road
Pownal, VT 05261

Cover photos:
Interior shot by COMSTOCK INC./Tom Grill
Window exterior by Henry W. Art
Cover design by Nancy Lamb
Design by Wanda Harper
Drawings by Wanda Harper
Edited by Constance Oxley and Deborah Burns
Typesetting by Hemmings Publishing
Printed in the United States by R.R. Donnelley & Sons Company

First Printing, August, 1987

Library of Congress Cataloging-in-Publication Data

Geiger, Richard H.
    Protect your home.

    "A Garden Way Publishing book."
    Includes index.
    1. Dwellings — Security measures. 2. Burglar-alarms.
I. Title.
TH9745.D85G45   1987   643'.16   87-45010
ISBN 0-88266-500-6
ISBN 0-88266-501-4 (pbk.)

Protect
Your Home
A Common-Sense
Guide to Home
Security

Acknowledgments

The author acknowledges with appreciation information furnished by the following people and organizations: CIGNA Corporation, Mr. Michael R. Bailey, Esq., National Association of Town Watch, Inc., and Matt A. Peskin.

Quote on p. 101 from Herrington, Lois H. Letter to Matt A. Peskin, 29 July 1985. U.S. Department of Justice, Office of the Assistant Attorney General.

Quote on p. 101 from Peskin, Matt A. Letter to author, 2 October 1986.

Quote on p. 102 from Pollock, Dr. John C. "The Figgie Report, Reducing Crime in America: Successful Community Effort." *The Police Chief,* December 1983.

Quote on p. 101 from Reagan, Ronald. *Proclamation: National Crime Watch Day.* Washington: Government Printing Office, August 12, 1986.

Quote on p. 106 from Rees, Fred H. *Investigators and Adjusters Handbook.* New York: The Spectator Company, 1926.

I dedicate this book to my wife, Peg, and my children, Scott, Ryan, and Lisa, without whose love and support I could not have written it.

Contents

Introduction

Right now you are probably thinking one of two things. One is that you'll read some of this book, but you know that you're never really going to be burglarized. The other is, "Why didn't I do something to protect my home *before* I was burglarized?" Yes, that's right. Statistics show that a majority of the people purchasing alarm equipment are doing so because they have already been burglarized or have had an attempted burglary of their home.

Do you know someone who has been burglarized? Was it a friend, neighbor, or maybe even a relative? How close did the burglar come to your home?

One of the first things that we all must admit is that installing an alarm system or taking other protective actions for your home is a lot like losing weight. It's something that many of us know we should do, but it's too much effort so we simply put it off until tomorrow. The real problem is that *tomorrow* may be the day that the burglar will pick *your home* to ransack.

There is one advantage that taking protective actions for your home has over weight control. Weight control is something we have to do every day for the rest of our lives. Once you've taken protective actions or installed an alarm system there is really very little to do to keep these items functioning.

The reason I have written this book is that I am just like you. I became interested in home security several years ago when my home was burglarized. I had only been in my new home a short time and had considered installing some sort of home security system, but everything seemed so complicated and expensive that I was afraid to make a mistake. I was also strapped for money after the purchase of my new home.

A short time later our first child arrived and home security devices were the furthest things from my mind. Even our dog, all 100 pounds, didn't know what to make of *this* noisy intruder.

On the second night home, our baby awoke at about 2 a.m. for his feeding. The dog jumped to his feet and started to growl. We thought that the baby's cries frightened him so we closed him in our bedroom. We went into our baby's room for his feeding. When we returned to our bedroom the dog was still quite upset, but we simply told him to go lie down and be quiet.

The next morning I went downstairs and felt a cold draft. I found the sliding glass doors of our family room standing wide open. When we checked further we found my wife's pocketbook lying on the floor. The contents were scattered about and the little bit of money that she had was gone. A large, crudely made knife was lying beside the pocketbook. Then a memory of the day before hit us. We had gone to church that day and my wife wore her new fox stole. She had hung it up in the closet in the hall but had forgotten to take it upstairs that night. You guessed it — it was gone. That stole had much more than monetary value. It had been purchased with money I had received for a suggestion that had saved money for my company. It was a complete surprise to my wife and something I probably would have never been able to justify from the family budget. Even if the insurance company were to replace it, it just wouldn't be the same. My wife would always remember that the new stole was not the special surprise she had loved so much.

The next thing we had to deal with was our own emotions. Someone had violated the security of our home. An unknown intruder had been in our house. Would he return? If so, would we be home again or would my wife be alone with the baby? We couldn't stop thinking about the knife. What would have happened if one of us had gone downstairs and surprised the burglar in the act? The thought was terrifying.

Although this burglary occurred several years ago, we have not yet recovered. Even with our security system my wife admits that she feels much more secure than before it was installed, but she still wonders what every noise is when I'm not at home.

You might wonder what happened to solve this crime. Well, we live in a small town with what I believe is an excellent police force. They responded to our call immediately and began their investigation. The investigating officer was very polite and also very honest. He admitted that it would have to be a stroke of luck to catch the thieves. The police theorized that the thief was already in the house when the baby awoke crying. They said that since there were no signs of forced entry he probably came through the sliding glass doors, which we had more than likely forgotten to lock. He probably rifled the pocketbook first, then moved into the hall where he was checking out the closet. The baby's crying brought us into the upstairs hall, causing him to flee with the stole and the money.

Because of my television "education" I immediately asked if the police were going to take fingerprints. Their reply was that this is only done for more serious crimes and then by the county crime unit. They said also that even if this crime had occurred in a large city the police probably would not take fingerprints because of the tremendous workload of more serious crimes. So much for my television education. We never recovered anything and the crime was never solved.

My first reaction was that I could put on all new locks the next day. Then I remembered that we had forgotten to lock the ones we had in the first place. You might be thinking that we were careless. Well, let's be honest. Do you always remember to lock all of your doors and windows? How many are locked right now? Take a walk around your home and see. Don't blame it on the kids. We are all human and forget to do these things. Statistics show that the majority of break-ins occur through unlocked or opened doors or windows. Most of the cars stolen each year are unlocked or even have the keys in them.

There was another attempted burglary of our home a short time later. Yes, I said attempted burglary. Our alarm system apparently frightened off the burglar. When the police arrived all they found was a sounding alarm and an opened door that was apparently jimmied.

The experience of a burglary isn't something that you would wish on your worst enemy. You are so angry you start to regret that you hadn't caught the thief in the act. You would have killed him! Would you? Or would he have killed you? Instead of wasting time on what I might have done, I began an in-depth investigation of security devices. There sure was a lot to learn and I don't claim to know everything. There are also people in the security field who disagree with me, but what I will tell you here are the things you can do with the smallest investment. Anyone can tell you how to spend lots of money. As I worked with the professionals in the field I learned what to do and what not to do.

I realized that other people were all going through the same thing I had gone through. They wanted to know what they should do. Who could they ask who didn't have a vested interest or would not try to sell them some device or system? Which system was right for their home? Who were the best installers? What could be done to improve home security without spending a great deal of money?

The entire purpose of this book is to give you enough information to allow you to make intelligent decisions about what to do in home security, whether to buy an alarm system or not, what type of system is best for you, and how to limit the impact of that system on both your lifestyle and your pocketbook.

If I've written this book correctly, most of those answers can be found right here. I did not intend this book to be a work of literature and am no threat to Mickey Spillane. Instead, what I have tried to do is to ask myself all those questions that have been asked of me over the years and give answers in plain English. This book will save you money if you read it. You should have enough information to understand what is needed to improve the security in your home whether it's the installation of an entire alarm system or just some of the improvements that I have outlined in Chapter 13. **Remember — it's too late to prevent the burglary that happened today — TOMORROW!**

1 | Should I Consider an Alarm System?

The question of whether or not to install an alarm system is one that many people struggle with every day. There are many things to consider and even some things that can be done if you don't have an alarm system.

First, you should know what an alarm system can and cannot do. An alarm system can be relatively simple and require virtually no participation by you. Or, it can be extremely sophisticated and turn your home into a virtual Fort Knox.

You must be careful. Every device you add to the basic system not only makes the system more expensive but it also makes it more complicated, increases maintenance problems, and may increase your false-alarm rate.

Let's examine the reasons for installing an alarm system, what you think your goal should be, and what it should *really* be. You might think that it's wise to catch the burglar in the act but what does this do for you? Probably nothing. What your goal should really be is to acquire an alarm system that helps prevent major losses and damage and is easy to live with. You should want the restrictions placed on you and your family, including the use of your home, to be as minimal as possible. It's not very logical to have a system that requires a degree in engineering to understand and forces your family to restrict their activities to one room of the home while the system is activated.

Alarm systems can range from simple ultrasonic tabletop models, which can be purchased in most electronic chain stores, to systems that could be used to protect the local bank or diamond exchange.

Costs for these systems are proportional to how much protection they provide and how sophisticated the protection is. The tabletop models often cost less than $100, while the more sophisticated systems can start at $1500 and extend into the $3000 range. Systems in banks and in diamond exchanges are many times more expensive than this figure.

There are basically three types of alarm systems. There are the ones that attempt to stop a burglar before he gets into your home. There are those that attempt to scare him off while letting everyone in the neighborhood know he has broken into your home. And there are the silent versions that attempt to catch the burglar in the act of burglarizing your home. I will discuss each of these in depth later in the book.

Now let's look at the advantages of having an alarm system. I guess I would have to admit that the major advantage is not really the actual security you get but the feeling of security you receive knowing that your alarm system is protecting you and your family while they are asleep. To attempt to tell you how much that feeling is worth in dollars would be useless. For example, if you were boating and accidentally fell out of the boat and were drowning, how much would the life preserver that someone threw you be worth? It actually cost less than $20 to purchase. How much would you have paid when you were gasping for air? See what I mean? Try asking someone who has experienced a burglary what they would have paid not to have to live with the fears they now have about it happening again. Ask if they feel the same about their home as they did before the burglary.

The next advantage is the actual security you receive. If a break-in does occur, what will be lost? Will it be simply money? Something that can be replaced? Or will it be your diamond engagement ring that was handed down to you from your grandmother and can't be replaced? Sure, the insurance company might give you enough money to purchase another diamond ring just as large as the one that was stolen. But is it the same as the one that was your grandmother's? If someone breaks in while you're at home asleep, will someone be injured?

One of the things every psychologist and criminologist knows is that when times get tough and the economy is in a slump, crime increases dramatically. All the economic experts say that we are going to see continuing increases in inflation and joblessness. All the criminologists say that serious crime will increase also. Do you want to become one of the percentage points in this year's increase?

Another advantage is that an alarm system can compensate for human failings like forgetfulness. Just think how many times you have gone out of the house and left doors and windows either opened or unlocked. Certainly the system won't remind you to lock them, but it will require that you close them before it can be armed. Now the only opportunity a burglar can take advantage of is if you simply don't turn on the alarm system.

There is a small indirect advantage offered by an alarm system — the discount on fire and theft insurance offered by some insurance companies. If you have an alarm system and are not getting a discount from your insurance company, I would shop around to find one at the same rate that offers a discount. Several companies are now offering them.

The rest of the justification is up to you. You are the final deciding factor in determining whether or not to install an alarm system. Only you know what the crime rate is in your neighborhood, what feeling of comfort you will get back, and how much you want to protect your family and possessions.

Please don't let my references to family mislead you. If you are single, you may have more of a need for an alarm system than someone married with a family. The reason is that single people offer a more predictable pattern of living. If you are at work a burglar doesn't have to worry about your wife, husband, or children coming home while he is burglarizing your home. He is fairly certain that you will be gone all day. It is also rare that a single person would have a dog or even neighbors who would notice something unusual going on around your home. Single people should also give careful consideration to installing an alarm system. They are easy prey for any burglar.

Because there are many aspects of alarm systems that you are unaware of, I have written this book in a question and answer format. Most of the questions asked of me over the years are answered here. The book is cheap compared to the losses you will incur from a break-in. If you make an uneducated purchase of an alarm system from a con artist, you will lose not only your money but a good portion of your sanity. A poorly functioning alarm system is the only thing worse than no alarm system at all. Just remember, it's not logical to expect to be able to buy an alarm system that can be installed with virtually no work, in minutes, at a very low cost, and still provide good protection.

I just hope that you are not reading this book because you are one of the many people who have already been burglarized. A great majority of the people who purchase alarm systems each day in the U.S. do so because they *have* been burglarized. If you haven't been burglarized yet, you should definitely read on and try to prevent this experience. If you are one of the unfortunate ones, you already know what I'm talking about. You must also read on and see how to best prevent this from ever happening again.

2 | Can I Prevent the Professional Burglar From Breaking In?

Before you determine whether you can prevent the professional burglar from getting into your home, you should determine whether this is a realistic concern for you. How wealthy are you? If you have an income over $100,000 a year and keep expensive jewels, collections, or other very valuable items in your home then you should be concerned about the professional.

The professional burglar, by definition, makes his living from burglarizing and not getting caught. He belongs to all the right clubs: the local yacht club, Kiwanis, Rotary, golf club. He might have even had a few drinks with you already. During these brief encounters, he will, as any friendly person would, discuss his collections and hobbies, such as stamp and coin collections, investments that he has made. You would probably respond, in an effort to be friendly and add to the conversation, with mention of things that you have done. He might even talk about a recent purchase of jewelry he made for his wife. The whole time he has a hidden objective — to assess your worth and determine if you have large amounts of valuables at home.

Next his conversation will turn to the problems associated with protecting this wealth from thieves. He might comment that he finds it inconvenient to go to the bank each time his wife wants to wear some of her jewelry so he has had a wall safe installed. He might even tell you how cleverly he has hidden it. You can't let this guy top you, so you tell him how much more clever you are by hiding your wife's valuables in a frozen food box in the freezer.

Then the game is "Can you top this?." You tell him about the minisafe in your bedroom that looks just like an outlet.

He keeps manufacturing problems and you and your friends keep helping him with your solutions. The best professionals join stamp and coin clubs. They hold the same type of conversations and even bring in and show some rather rare items just to spur on the game.

Someone might object at this point that I have used the word *he* all through this book when describing a burglar. This is only the generic "he." If you don't believe that there are some top women burglars out there you are mistaken. Many teams of men and women work the better clubs. Also, when I refer to your *wife's* valuables, the valuables can also be your husband's, a partner's, or a roommate's.

Often the conversation revolves around his alarm system and how confusing its features are or problems that he has had with it. Again in an effort not to be outdone and to help, you tell him everything that he needs to know about your alarm system.

Unless you fit the previous description, the professional is never going to hit your home. The professional isn't going to risk five to ten years in jail for a Sony portable color T.V. If the professional burglar wanted to get into your home there is probably no alarm system you could afford that could stop him. Yes, that's right, even the most sophisticated systems can be beaten by a "pro." All that has to be done is to make the prize worth his trying.

Now you are probably wondering why you should consider an alarm system if the pro isn't interested in your home. The reason is that over 90 percent of all the break-ins committed each year are of the hit-and-miss variety. They are committed by amateurs or at most semi-professionals.

Again, we provide the opportunities for these people, too. Here's how.

Many of us, again in an attempt to be helpful, provide all the information a burglar needs to carry out his goals. Let's take a few examples. Let's suppose you are in the shower or otherwise indisposed and the telephone rings. You are unable to get to it in time although it rings quite a long time. About ten minutes later, your doorbell rings. You begin to get halfway presentable and next you hear someone pounding on your door. By the time you get dressed and downstairs the person has moved around to the back door and resumed his pounding.

You open the door and there is a young man you have never seen before. He asks if this is the Johnston residence. You know that the Johnstons live several doors up the street, so you tell him he has the wrong house. He apologizes profusely and goes on his way. Except for your dismay about being disturbed, you think nothing of what happened.

Let's examine what might have just happened. The young man at your door had driven down the street and read the Johnston name off the mailbox several doors down the street (so convenient, isn't it?). After getting your name off your mailbox and your address off your home he went to a local phone, called information, and got your telephone number. He called from the booth to see if anyone was home. That was the persistent call you missed. After completing the first test, he went to your front door. He rang the bell and almost pounded it down. Your slow response sent him around to the back door where he repeated his act.

If a neighbor had seen him and challenged him he would have used the same story on him that he used on you. Your neighbor would have most likely fallen for it also.

You were lucky today. You answered the door so he went to another street and repeated his little charade.

If you hadn't answered the attempts he made at the two doors, he would have tried the doorknob to see if it was unlocked. Most entries are through unlocked doors. He would then have tried the sliding glass doors or any window or door through which he could gain access without drawing attention to himself. Depending on how close your neighbors' homes were and what type of privacy he had, the next step would be to break in. He would simply kick the door open. On most doors this is very successful. If this failed he would use something that you have sitting right there for his use: gardening tools, regular tools, firewood, or potted plants. He would break a pane of glass or even the door itself.

Now that he is in, he will listen for any strange sounds — a radio, singing, a dog, or anything that might indicate that someone is at home. He'll then open up the largest door near him and leave it open for rapid escape. He will probably go first to the family room to see what can be had there easily. He might take a quick stop in the kitchen checking any teapots or sugar bowls for money. Next it's straight to the master bedroom. This is the room that usually has the money, jewelry, or guns.

If he has a car he probably parked it right out front, but just down the street a little way. He will then probably go right out the front door with everything he has in some brown bags. He might even have the nerve to turn and wave just in case someone is watching. he would use the back exit if it gave him better concealment and would not present some obstacle to him carrying his booty.

Now that I have described the method which, with some slight variations, represents the majority of break-ins in the U.S. each year, you can see why it is so successful.

This is the type of break-in that you should be trying to prevent. The professional wouldn't even consider your home or mine. He knows before he even gets into a home just what he is going to find and what it is worth to him.

With this in mind, I believe you will agree that the type of burglary we should concern ourselves with in this book is that done by the amateur or semi-pro.

3 | What Are the Primary Goals of an Alarm System?

Every good alarm system should meet three primary goals. It should:

1. Make a great deal of noise both inside and outside the home.
2. Light the interior and possibly the exterior of the home.
3. Do the first two things in a reliable manner with a low false-alarm rate.

The First Goal

Let's examine the first goal: Making lots of noise inside and outside of the home. It's extremely important to make lots of noise because the burglar relies on the fact that no one knows he is there. Not only should he hear the alarm so that he knows he is in trouble, but everyone in the neighborhood should know he is in the home. Even in remote areas, where there is little chance of anyone hearing an alarm, there should be loud noises because this will scare the burglar. He would not want to take the chance that someone else will hear it. The purpose is as much to scare the burglar as to notify your neighbors of the break-in. In very remote areas this system should be backed up with a telephone dialer that would call the police when the entry occurs.

Most modern dialers will continue to call the police until someone at the police station answers. Some dialers will even call the police for illegal entry and the fire company for a fire alarm. A dialer can cost $200 or more. At this cost, noise might be the only option for some people.

The next problem is to determine the method to make this noise. The method becoming more and more popular today is electronic sirens. The reason for this innovation is that they take very little current to operate and will, therefore, run for a long time on a battery backup system. These sirens make either a wailing or a steady sound similar to the sirens used on emergency vehicles.

I must admit that I'm not tremendously thrilled about the use of electronic sirens because they do sound like those used in emergency vehicles. All too often, people mistake these for an ambulance. Because of this confusion precious minutes are lost in reporting a crime in process. If at all possible a mechanical bell should be used. This sound is distinctly the sound of a burglar alarm. It should be noted that bells do draw considerably more operating current for their operation; therefore they must have a suitable battery backup. Bells also require a weatherproof housing so that birds and bees do not make nests in them. This could cause the bell to either be muffled or malfunction completely. In areas where it is necessary to have the alarm sound for a long time before someone might hear the sound, it would be wiser to use an electronic siren. In rural areas, time is lost merely by the fact that not many people are around to hear the alarm and call the police. As I said before, it might be wise to use a telephone dialer in these more remote areas. Still, use the electronic siren simply to frighten the burglar away before damage can be done to your property.

You should always combine an exterior alarm with an interior alarm. You might think the burglar is surely going to hear that loud siren outside the house, but that's not necessarily true. Sound is very susceptible to wind direction and weather. If there is a strong wind the sound could be carried away enough to make it difficult to hear inside the home. You must be sure the burglar knows he has set off an alarm. He must also know that everyone else knows he has broken into your home. This could prevent additional losses or damage that might occur if he thought that his entry went undetected. You must also know there has been a burglary. If you are asleep, in the shower, or have on a stereo headset, surely you would like to know that you have an uninvited guest in your home.

One of the most convenient methods of distributing the sound around your home is to install a small electronic siren inside the air duct of the hot air or air-conditioning system. This will send the sound to every room. If you don't have ducts in your home, place the siren in the attic, basement, or both if necessary. The need for both locations must be determined after you see how well the sound gets through your home.

The Second Goal

The second goal is to light both the interior and exterior of the home. Most homes have some form of main lighting in the foyer or kitchen area that can light most of the first floor. If, in your case, it is the kitchen light, this is the one to tie into your alarm system. Select a permanent light fixture so that the burglar can not merely unplug it to extinguish the light. By lighting the downstairs area, you have removed one of the burglar's greatest allies — darkness. He will flee faster because of this than because of the noise. The reason is twofold. First, if there is a light you might be able to see him to identify him to the police. Second, neighbors can see the lights on in your home and if they know that you are out or away this will cause them to call the police.

The reason for lighting the exterior is virtually the same as for the interior. If the burglar has been caught in the process of opening a door or window, he will immediately duck down behind the beautiful shrubs that we all so conveniently plant so close to the house. When the exterior lights come on he will have no choice but to run or be caught. This lighting can be accomplished in most cases by merely using the existing exterior lights. They can be turned on by an auxiliary contact in the central control box of the alarm system. A wire from your system can activate a relay that will control the lights in the same manner as the switch does. This will not interfere with the normal use of these lights.

If you don't have any exterior lighting, I heartily recommend that you install some. If you install spotlights on all four corners of your home, you will be able to light the entire outside at once. When a forced entry occurs you are at the mercy of the burglar if there is no additional lighting. How will you know where he is hiding? He will most certainly know where you are. In most homes the light switch controlling the outside lights is not located in such a way as to allow the owner to operate them without going through the home into the back room, work room, or laundry room. This is normally the same for the interior lights. Most hall switches are located in the center or at the ends of the upstairs hall. This requires that the owner come out into the hall and risk personal injury in order to turn on the lights.

Even if you aren't going to install an elaborate alarm system, I recommend that you at least install switches that control both the main hall lights and the exterior lights from the master bedroom. Can you remember how many times you have heard a noise outside your home in the middle of the night? You get to the window in the dark, after breaking your toe on the leg of the bed.

You raise the shade and look outside only to find that there isn't enough light to see an intruder even if he were waving the American flag on your lawn. Wouldn't it be convenient if you could throw a switch from your bedroom to turn on the outside lights? This might not only help you sleep better, but it would also tend to cut down on vandalism.

The Third Goal

The third goal of a good alarm system is reliability. This simply means accomplishing the first two goals in a reliable manner. Having no alarm system at all is not as bad as having one that is constantly triggering false alarms.

Try to picture yourself in bed early in the morning. It's pitch dark and all of a sudden your alarm goes off. You leap into some state that resembles consciousness. It takes some time to get your bearings and realize that the loud noise you hear is your alarm system. No matter who you are, you are frightened! You immediately think of your family so you run into their bedrooms, grab them out of a sound sleep, and haul them into your room to safety. During the minutes that follow, everything that you've ever seen on T.V. or in the movies concerning crime, goes through your mind. Where is the burglar? What will he do? Will he come upstairs? Do I have a weapon I can use? Will the police ever get here? Those minutes seem like hours. Your heart is pounding, the kids are crying, and finally the police arrive. This could have been a record response time for them but no one could ever convince you. You are so excited the first thing you yell to them is, "Where have you been? We could have all been killed by the time you got here."

How would you feel now if this were a false alarm? After checking the entire premises the police find nothing. There never was a burglar. How would you feel if this weren't the first time? This is not at all uncommon. I have often spoken with people with this same problem. They are either trying to live with a system that is constantly giving false alarms or have completely disabled their alarm system.

You might say now, "See, I told you that those alarm systems aren't worth a nickel!" Wrong. This problem will not occur if you select your system from the industry leaders in alarm equipment. Have it installed by a firm with a proven track record or install it yourself following all directions carefully. Do not try to make your alarm system so extravagant that it becomes a monster to live with. Of the many systems I have installed, I have never had a problem with false alarms and neither do the large commercial installation companies. If they did they wouldn't be in business today.

False alarms can cause you to lose faith in your system. They will irritate both the neighbors and the police. This problem has gotten so severe in some areas due to the "fly-by-night" systems and installers that many police departments have adopted a false-alarm fine. This fine is levied against anyone who has a system that has more than a set number of false alarms. You don't want to become the victim of the "cry wolf syndrome." If this happens and a real burglary occurs, either your neighbors won't report it or the police won't respond as quickly.

Stopping the Burglar

There are many manufacturers out there claiming their systems can stop the burglar before he ever gets into your home. I'm sure that you've seen the ads. There are just as many methods used to try to accomplish this task. The problem is that it is difficult to distinguish between a burglary attempt, a kid walking through your backyard, a tree limb falling against the side of your home, or even loud noises like a clap of thunder.

The difference between a burglar hitting his shoulder into the door and a large tree limb falling onto the premises is very difficult to determine. Naturally, companies selling these devices will tell you that these sounds are distinctly different and that their systems can tell them apart. I will not argue that the sound patterns made by breaking glass or wood may be completely different than those made by the falling tree limb. The real problem is that there isn't enough of a difference to insure that you won't get enough false alarms to upset both you and the neighborhood. Not one of these companies has a guarantee stating their system will not make this mistake.

Let's take a simple example. Suppose you are home at night alone and have the system on for protection, which is logical. You are doing the dishes and you accidentally drop a glass. The alarm system interprets this as a break-in attempt and starts sounding the sirens. Is this acceptable? You might agree that this was a correct operation, but would you be able to convince your neighbor whose baby was awakened and is now screaming? Sometimes these systems respond to harmonics (multiples) of the trigger frequencies. This could be caused by any number of things, from thunder to the operation of an electronic garage-door opener. Even surges in the electrical system can also trigger some detectors.

I think it is acceptable to require that there is an actual attempt at opening a door or window to set off an alarm. Using this theory alone will reduce false alarms to the point where they are virtually nonexistent.

Silent Alarms

In a silent alarm system when a break-in occurs the system will alarm but no audible sound will be made. Usually the purpose for this type of system is that if an audible sound is made, the burglar out of anger might injure the person responsible for setting off the alarm. It is for this reason that silent alarms are often used in banks, bars, and other commercial facilities where an armed robbery might occur. At this time the alarm system can be triggered without the knowledge of the burglar.

Many times, dialers are used in silent alarm systems. A dialer is simply a mechanical device that when triggered dials a preset telephone number, usually the number of the local police. It then plays a prerecorded message stating that a robbery is taking place at the following address. Some systems have two tapes, one for a burglary and one for fire. These systems are more expensive than a plain local alarm and they do, on occasion, have some problems. Mechanical failures are very low, however, and the systems seem reliable.

One problem with dialers is that they will also call the police when you have made a mistake and open a door with the system armed without realizing it. This is why most police departments will telephone the residence or business first to see if everything is in order before dispatching a cruiser.

You might think that since you pay the police officer's salary he would respond anyway. Remember, in every town there are only so many police or firefighters. If they are responding to a false alarm at your home while a real robbery is taking place in another location, someone could get seriously hurt or even killed.

Another more commercial system is one that uses a direct connection to the police station. In this system a company rents you a device that will cause an alarm to sound at the local police station when there is a break-in at your residence. These systems are very reliable but have high rental charges that are often more than the average owner can justify. With these systems, the police will normally telephone your home or business and expect a reply. This reply must use a predetermined code number or phrase that will tell them if this is really an alarm or just an accident.

A variation on this system is one that sounds an alarm at the location of the rental company's security building. In some instances these companies have their own guard forces who respond, or they simply call the police and report that there has been an alarm. It is not unusual for this type of system to be used mainly for commercial use where the expense can be written off against the cost of operating the business.

The real mentality to avoid is the one that says that it is your job to catch the burglar. I disagree very much. I think that it is your responsibility to protect your family and property and to leave catching the criminals to those people who are professionally trained to do the job — the police.

If you really feel that the police are understaffed (in most cases this is true), you should join a Town Watch Program. These programs have proven their worth across the nation by reducing crime in the areas where they are properly staffed. They provide the police with the most valuable tool they can have — hundreds of extra eyes and ears.

If none of these programs exist in your area, start one. The police would be delighted to assist you. There is also a National Town Watch Association. They will be very helpful in getting you started in the right direction. These programs do not involve you in any direct confrontation with criminals and do not require a great deal of your time. (See Chapter 14.)

You may hear from your friends that the average monetary loss in the U.S. for a single burglary is about $500. This is true. Your friends might argue that this isn't enough to justify an expensive alarm system. There are some pitfalls in using these national averages. Whenever you use an average you must remember that there are a number of people who have suffered losses above the average and a number who have had losses below this figure. You know your luck. Which end would you get you would be on? National figures also tend to distort the picture for any given area. For instance, the losses in a rural area might be significantly different than those that occur in a large city.

The real problem comes not in the actual value of an item stolen but in the value of that item to you. What value would you place on the first little gold ring that you received from a loved one? This value would most certainly exceed that of the true dollar value of the gold and more than exceed the value placed on it by the insurance company.

Your intent in having an alarm system should not be to eliminate all losses entirely, although this would be ideal. What it should be is to reduce those losses by limiting the loss of property and preventing any harm from occurring to you or your family. To try to put a monetary value on the feeling of security that you receive from an alarm system would be ridiculous. Each person must decide for himself what the value would be and no two people will agree.

4 | What are the Types of Alarm Systems?

In this chapter, I will discuss the most common types of alarm systems and list the advantages and disadvantages of each. A system that might not be suitable for the average owner might be excellent for a commercial or industrial use and vice versa.

Modular Systems

A modular system is any system that comes as an entire unit, ready to operate. It usually operates from a standard A.C. outlet. In only a few cases does it have a battery backup to protect against a loss of power. There are an enormous number of these systems.

The reason there are so many kinds of modular systems is first, that the problem of burglary is very great, and second, they appeal to the average person. They require little or no installation, virtually no knowledge of electronics or wiring, and usually have very low costs. Ah! The panacea. Is this really the answer to your nightmares?

It is true that these systems are usually lower in cost, but cost many times is a reflection of quality. You cannot expect the same degree of protection and flexibility from these systems as you will get from a hard-wired system.

Most modular systems use some form of motion detection to allow them to protect a large area with a single unit. In most motion detection systems, a beam is sent out and reflects from any solid object. The reflected beam is then received by the same unit and compared electronically to the transmitted beam. If the object was stationary, the reflected beam and the transmitted beam will be the same. If the reflecting object was in motion, the reflected beam would be different from the transmitted beam. This difference would trigger an alarm. It makes little difference what the size of the object is. All objects large and small will act the same. This characteristic of motion detection causes these systems to have a very high rate of false alarms.

The advantages of these systems are fairly obvious. They do not require any sophisticated installation. They can be removed easily and taken with the owner if the home is sold. They are comparatively cheap. If service is needed they can be taken to a service agency (if one exists). It may be possible to send them back to the manufacturer.

Now for the disadvantages. Except for a few systems that accept external contacts, most modular systems can only protect one general area (e.g., living room, main hall). [This might not be a disadvantage depending on the construction of your home]. If an intruder were to come in through a window in a room that was not protected by the unit's beam, he would not be detected unless he went into the area that the system protects.

These systems are "active systems." They do not allow anyone to enter the protected area. For this reason they cannot be used while anyone is in the protected area. It is common for animals and small children to set off these alarms. Some of these systems use ultrasonic sound waves. These are sounds that are above normal human hearing range. You should be careful that the frequency used is not one that will drive your pets crazy. Animals have a much higher hearing range than do humans and some ultrasonic sound waves will disturb them. These systems usually have a self-contained siren or buzzer as the alarm device that generally cannot be heard outside the home. When a burglar trips the alarm, he will run out only to discover that he is the only one who could hear it. Upon making this discovery he will return and disable the system. Just to add insult to injury, there have been several cases where the thief also stole the modular system.

The smallest movement will set off these alarms. Sometimes the owner isn't even aware of these movements, such as the sway of a drape in a breeze, or the movement of an article when heat comes on. Some systems use frequencies that will reach right through thin partitions and detect motion on the other side or even through glass, for example, detecting the movement of a bush outside the home. It is easy to see why the false-alarm rate is so high.

Commercial Systems with 24-Hour Guard Service

Without a doubt, these systems are usually the most elaborate and expensive. They are also probably the best systems. They are usually hard-wired and are backed up by a private guard service. These guards operate in two modes. One type of service will simply call the police when there is an alarm at your residence. The other will actually dispatch their own guards and the police to your residence. In some areas of the country, people must depend on the state police to respond to an alarm at their residence. This is because they do not have a local police force. The state police do the best job possible, but they have very large areas to patrol and might not be available when your alarm system goes off.

Systems that use a private guard service are usually installed by the company's own professional installers. These people are installing systems on a daily basis and have seen virtually every problem. They are skilled technicians whose work is virtually invisible. The system itself is normally of the most sophisticated and reliable design. This is to minimize false alarms. It would be unwise for these companies to install systems that are constantly triggering false alarms. Their guards would be running all over the place for nothing.

They operate in the following manner. When an alarm occurs, a signal alerts a central office, usually through a radio transmitter or private telephone line. A guard at the central office immediately telephones your residence to determine if it is a mistake on your part. When you answer, he expects to hear a prearranged code phrase. If this phrase is missing or no one answers, he dispatches his guard force and alerts the police.

On arrival at your home they check out the entire premises. If there was a break-in they check to see if anything on their list of valuables is missing and alert you of the problem. They then restore the home and system to normal and leave.

There are a few drawbacks. The first and largest is cost. This type of system is usually the most expensive and it becomes difficult for the average person to justify it, unless he is rich or can write it off to his business. There is a constant monthly service charge for the system. If the owner accidentally trips the system he will receive a call from the service — a small inconvenience for this degree of protection. When you are going out you may be required to call the service so that they will know how to reach you, in case of emergency. Some people even fear that the guards will have a list of your valuables and therefore know what to steal or be able to tell someone else. I don't support this concern at all. These firms have been in business for many years and are careful in selecting their guards. They would be the first to detect a bad apple. After all, this means the reputation of their company and therefore its profit.

Please don't misread my support of these firms as an advertisement. I'm neither employed by one nor do I own stock in one. I simply believe that quality should be recognized where it exists as quickly as lack of quality should be pointed out.

Commercial Systems without Guard Service

Systems installed by professionals like ADT (see Manufacturers, p. 145) are certainly the best way to go, but unfortunately, they are also more expensive than doing it yourself. I believe that many people have enough talent to install a comparable system and save a great deal of money. The major problem is that it will take several days or even weeks to install a good hard-wired system and some people believe that this is too much effort.

If you are going to use a commercial alarm service, I recommend that you stay with one of the large established services that have a reputation built over many years. There are too many owners who decide to use a local guy who gave them a great price. Later they find out that he is no longer in business, and their system is malfunctioning to the point where it is worthless.

A good commercial alarm service has many advantages and virtually no disadvantages except for greater cost. They are neat installers and generally supply state-of-the-art equipment. They are rapid to respond to any problem and quick to resolve it.

Systems Tied Directly to the Police Station

Many systems often referred to as central-station systems have direct indications at the local police station. There is a monthly service charge for the rental of the communicating device. There must also be sufficient room available on the display panel of the police station before you can acquire an indicating unit.

These systems are certainly useful where the home is located in a remote area where there is little chance of a local alarm being heard and reported. This system would alert the police directly. Many commercial and industrial uses select this option. The major objection I have to this type of system is when it is coupled to a silent alarm. Some owners install a central-station system and have no local alarm (bell or siren). This is done in an attempt to catch the burglars. I don't believe that it is either wise or your responsibility to try to catch a burglar, but simply to frighten him away.

The direct alerting systems have the same problems that the commercially monitored systems have — you must notify the police when there is a false alarm. Many areas of the country have passed ordinances requiring the owner to pay a penalty charge to the police department in the event they are required to respond to a false alarm at your residence. This is easily justified because if the police are at your residence on a false alarm, they may not be able to respond to a real emergency. With the large number of cheap systems on the market, and those that are poorly installed, false alarms could become a real problem.

Your Own Residential Alarm System

The best method of protecting your family and home, in my opinion, is to install a good electronic alarm system that meets the criteria set forth in Chapter 6. It might first appear that this is a huge undertaking, but the comfort that the system provides will make the effort of the installation worth your time.

In most situations, a system that sounds a local alarm will be sufficient. The more unusual your security situation the more you can justify the additional costs of a more sophisticated system. Be sure to plan out the system and installation well. If you choose to have the system installed by a professional, take the steps I have outlined in Chapter 9. Just don't be surprised if you don't follow the suggested steps and use a company of "rip-off artists," that you find it impossible to get another company to straighten out the problems. The attitude of most companies is that they would rather install another new system entirely rather than try to figure out what someone else did wrong.

5 | How Flexible Can an Alarm System Be?

If you are asking, "Will I have to be a prisoner in my home to get good protection?", I can say that it isn't necessary to be a prisoner for a system to be considered good. If you happen to be the type of person who wants an alarm system that is the equivalent of the one used at Fort Knox, you will be a prisoner in your home. I will stress all through this book that the best alarm systems are those that accomplish the primary goals of an alarm system without restricting your normal life-style to the point where you begin to feel like a prisoner.

There must be reason to all things. You cannot expect to have a system that will require absolutely no change in your present life-style. If this is the case, take my advice and don't waste your money or time no matter what the salesperson tells you the system can do. There is no system made that will provide any acceptable degree of protection without having some impact on the manner in which you use your home. For some people these changes are difficult to make. For others, who are more security conscious, they won't require much, if any, change in their style of living. Let's discuss some of the changes you might have to make, depending on the type of alarm system that you select.

The Active System

Active systems detect the presence of an individual, his motion in a given area, or his contact with a certain object. They are unable to discriminate between the owner and an intruder; therefore, they have certain problems in their application. These systems by definition restrict movement for both you and your pets in the protected area. If you have a sonic or infrared detection system in use inside your home, you will not be able to enter the protected areas when the system is armed (activated). You will have to disarm (deactivate) the system or restrict your movements while in the area to avoid the detection devices. You must always remember to avoid the protected areas when the system is armed. This can severely restrict either the use of your home or the use of your system. If you accidentally wander or allow your pets to enter the protected area, an alarm will go off. You must remember to turn the system off first thing in the morning or suffer the embarrassment of having the alarm system triggered because one of your children walked into the protective beam. You might want to use the protected area of your home in the evening while you are alone and therefore wish to have the alarm system on to provide protection. This would not be possible with the active system. There are some advantages of the active method of detection, such as ease of installation and the ability to protect a large area with a single device, but their applications must be carefully considered.

Even with the passive system you must remember to turn off the system before opening the doors or windows at night, but at least they require some conscious effort to set them off and they are prone to fewer false alarms. The passive system also allows you to enter into a protected area when the system is armed without setting off the alarm. Therefore, it gives you full protection even at night when you might wish to use the protected area.

With systems using motion, even the slightest movement, such as the swaying of a curtain, can cause an alarm. Even air currents from the heating system and sometimes movement of bushes on the other side of thin partitions, such as windows, can set off an alarm. Motion-detection systems and radar systems are similar; they both have a very high false-alarm rate and can be upset by things like spurious electronic signals or vibrations caused by heavy traffic or thunder. Of course the more expensive the system the fewer of these problems it exhibits. Some of the very expensive motion-detection systems have excellent false-alarm rates, but the cost is prohibitive to the average owner. These systems are not uncommon for commercial and industrial use where the facility has excellent control over motion, such as warehouses or drugstores.

In spite of the problems with motion-detection systems, they are extensively used in the commercial fields combined with sophisticated detection systems like "E" fields and proximity detectors. We won't get into these because this book is about home protection. Commercial protection is an entirely different field. Motion-detection systems can easily be employed in a large area with a minimum of equipment. They do not require a straight "line-of-sight" as does infrared. Often active systems are used in conjunction with passive systems in case the burglar manages to get through the first line of protection or if it fails in service. In the home, this combination could be employed when you are away on vacation in conjunction with your first zone of protection. By doing this, the owner gets both types of protection and can switch off the active system when at home, to gain greater flexibility.

The Passive System

The passive system, in my opinion, offers the best protection for the money in most residential applications. It is this type, therefore, that I most often recommend. The passive system has all the features of the active system with the exception that you can use the protected areas while the system is armed. This gives you a greater degree of freedom in your home.

In the passive system you must actually open the door or window to set off an alarm. All windows and doors are monitored separately. I admit that in most cases this does require a great deal of installation effort. But you only have to do this once. Once it is installed you must remember to shut all doors and windows before attempting to arm the system. You might think this a disadvantage, but you must remember that if you are to increase the security of your home, it is going to be difficult to accomplish with the doors and windows left open to invite the burglar to enter. With the number of homes that have air-conditioning, this isn't nearly the problem it was many years ago.

If you take the time to design and plan your system correctly you will be able to live inside a ring of protection while enjoying a rather normal life-style.

Proper Design of Your Passive System

A properly designed system should include:

A method of being armed and disarmed from the inside of the house, not the outside. This is because an outside control station provides a burglar with more opportunities than necessary and might tempt him to try to defeat the system by disassembling the control station. Although this can be easily prevented, control stations inside the home present fewer problems due to extremes in weather or possible tampering. With the inside control station a burglar is required to actually enter the protected area to get to the control station. This provides another chance that he will set off the alarm.

A simple method of turning the system on and off. Some systems offer digital control with a "punch pad" similar to a calculator. This requires memorizing a code number that will arm and disarm the system. Some designs will also lock you out if you make a mistake, requiring you to remember an unlock code before you will be allowed to try again. After a certain number of bad attempts the system will either alarm or lock out completely. This is to prevent a burglar from simply trying to guess the code by trying numbers at random. At first a punch pad seems like a good idea, but every device has its hidden surprises. For instance, what happens to the elderly person who, due to poor sight or coordination, makes too many mistakes? What about coming home some night slightly intoxicated and you can't for the life of you remember the number? Remember also that once you give the code to a friend or neighbor you can't simply ask for it back like a key. Don't let me mislead you. The codes can be changed but it's not very easy, and how many times do you want to memorize new codes?

I prefer either the flat or round key system. These keys have patented patterns and cannot be duplicated by the average locksmith. I think this is better security and more convenient even though it might be another key to carry. Keys can be duplicated, lost or stolen but we accept this risk every day with all of our keys.

A set of system status lights that tell the condition of the system. It should have a light to indicate whether the system is safe to arm (all windows and doors are closed) and a light telling you that the system *is* armed or *is not* armed. These lights are very helpful when trying to find the window or door that isn't closed.

Two zones of protection, one that is external (doors, windows, etc.) and one that is internal (interior doors, mats, infrared, etc.). This second zone allows you to use devices that you might not prefer to live with on a constant basis (e.g., infrared, ultrasonics, etc.) and still get the added protection of these devices when you are away on a trip. They will provide backup for the first zone of protection. That way if the burglar manages to get through the first zone he will get caught by the second zone.

A battery backup feature that automatically transfers the source of power from the power line 120 volt A.C. to the battery housed in the control box. This battery is constantly trickle-charged through the alarm system during normal operation. Many good alarm systems have been defeated simply because the power to the house was lost or cut. With the newer electrical codes requiring the installation of electric meters on the outside, it becomes very easy for a burglar to cut all the power to the home by simply pulling out the meter.

  A bell/siren cut-off timing circuit. This circuit would prevent the alarm from sounding indefinitely if the owner is away for some extended period of time. If an alarm keeps ringing constantly, the police, in an effort to restore peace to the neighborhood, must make some attempt to silence the disturbance. They will take whatever steps necessary. All too often this means damage to the system and maybe even damage to the home. Auto cut-off merely stops the bell/siren from sounding after a predetermined time and then resets the system to normal. This assumes that all doors and windows have been closed (the system has been returned to "normal").

  Built-in fire protection circuits. You might say that this adds to the expense. You are right but more people are killed in fires each year than from any other threat. You would have a difficult time finding an alarm system central control box that has all the other features that I have mentioned and doesn't have fire protection circuits. Statistically, fire protection is a much better investment.

  If the previous items are included in your system, you will have a system that offers years of protection in a reliable manner. If you are worried about the cost of it, simply divide the cost by at least ten years and then by the number of people in your home and you have the cost per person per year. This is a small sum to protect the life of people you love. You pay much more for insurance each year and get no better feeling of security after you've purchased it.

System Limitations

  There are some limitations that you can expect from just about any alarm system. In general they are:

  Most passive systems are hard-wired. These systems are the most expensive to have installed. You must remember that once the wires are installed you will never have to replace them, so it's a once-in-a-lifetime job. Because in a passive system almost all doors and windows are monitored, you must remember to close them every time you leave your home, if you intend to arm your system. At first this might seem to be a big problem especially when all that you want to do is take a short run over to the school or down the street to the store. You might think that you'll only be gone for a minute, but that type of carelessness is just what the average burglar depends on. If you think you would feel terrible if you were burglarized, just imagine how you would feel if you were burglarized because you were too lazy to close all the windows and doors and set the alarm before you went out.

How to get fresh air into the home. There is an accepted practice for accomplishing this goal but it weakens the system. Two magnets can be installed on those windows intended to be opened. One magnet is installed at the bottom of the window in its normal position and the other on the moving sash about six inches up from the bottom. The contact portion is also installed six inches up from the bottom of the window on the frame. Now when you wish to let in fresh air you line up the magnet that will allow a six-inch opening and then set the alarm. If anyone tries to come in through this window and moves it, the alarm goes off. Most installers agree that the distance should not exceed six inches or someone might be able to get in without opening the window further. You must also remember that you cannot get up in the middle of the night and shut the window. If you do, everyone in the neighborhood will know that you closed your window. Your alarm system will tell them, loud and clear.

If the system you install uses active detection devices such as motion detection, infrared, or mats, you will have to restrict the freedom that you allow your family and pets. If they accidentally wander into the protected area, they will set off the alarm. It won't take many of these false alarms to get your neighbors irritated.

Because you have to arm and disarm the system, you will either have to carry another key or memorize a code number. This will also require that you have someone in the neighborhood whom you will trust with your key. This is in case you are away and something happens at your home. They might have to shut off the alarm when the police have checked it out and returned it to normal. You will have to explain the system operation method to relatives and close friends whom you allow to enter using their own keys. Your children will have to be given a key and taught how to use the system.

You must avoid getting into the frame of mind where you say that it's not really necessary to lock your doors now because you have an alarm system. Just try to picture this sequence of events. You decide one day to go out with neighbors and go in their car. Your brother stops in to see you. Seeing your car in the driveway, he figures that you're home so he walks right in through the unlocked front door. The alarm system goes off and the police arrive. Can you see him trying to explain to the police that he is your brother? It could be very embarrassing. Not to mention that when doors are left unlocked it makes it that much easier for a burglar.

I felt an obligation to tell you some of the drawbacks in an alarm system. I hope that I didn't scare you! I have known many people both young and old who have alarm systems installed in their homes, and all of these people have become so comfortable with their systems that these problems don't really exist. Believe me when I tell you that after a short period of getting familiar with your system, you won't have problems like those mentioned either. Just don't expect the system to know the difference between a burglar coming in the back door and you. If the alarm is on and you go into a protected area it will treat you the same way that it treats the burglar.

6 | What are the Features of a Good Alarm System?

Self-Restoring

Every system should have a self-restoring feature. In the event that an alarm is triggered, it will restore itself to normal after a predetermined time. This is important because often a system will be triggered when the owner is not at home. The burglar is either frightened off or the police arrive to restore the residence to normal. After this occurs the alarm system should take up the process of protecting your property again. It is not unheard of for a burglar to attempt a break-in and when the alarm goes off, run away and hide until the system is disabled by the police, only to return after the police have left and complete the job.

Automatic Cutoff

The automatic cutoff is even more important than the self-restoring feature. When an alarm system is triggered your neighbors will accept the disturbance as a necessity to allow you to protect your home. If this system continues to sound endlessly into the night, the neighbors start to complain. The police will have no other choice but to make an attempt to silence the alarm in order to restore peace to the neighborhood. During these attempts, many alarm systems and homes have been damaged. Once this damage is done the system is nonfunctional and your home is open to burglary until you return. You should just pray that you are not away for an extended vacation.

A good system will sound the alarm for a preset period of time (usually about twenty minutes to half an hour) and then stop. The system will automatically reset (if all the doors and windows have been closed — the system is "normal") and take up the job of protecting your home once again. If any of the doors or windows are still left open or any of the sensing elements (contacts, tape, mats) are not "normal," the system will simply shut down completely.

Two Zones of Protection

I prefer a system that offers more than one "zone" of protection. A "zone" of protection is similar to a ring around your home. The first zone would be all the externally protected points while the second zone would be the interior points of protection. This second zone is often referred to as the "trap" zone because it may be the last chance your system will have to "trap" a burglar. If for some unknown reason he has managed to get through the first zone, the second zone detectors will more than likely trap him.

If you have a second zone you can get the advantages of both active and passive detection methods and minimize the disadvantages of the active methods. How, you might ask. Well, the active detection methods are in the second zone, which is only switched on when you are planning to be away for an extended period of time. This extended period might allow the more experienced burglar the time to figure out a way around your window contacts.

The burglar enters expecting to get past the window contacts and is caught by stepping onto a concealed mat that triggers the system (see Chapter 11). These active detection methods would cause problems by inhibiting the use of your home if they were in service all the time. By only using these detectors when you are away, the degree of protection that you receive is maximized.

Battery Throw-Over

A battery throw-over is a backup system for the normal A.C. electrical supply feeding your alarm system. There are occasions when the electric service is lost in your home. If your system relies entirely on electric service for power, it will not provide any protection at all during these times.

With a battery throw-over system, when the electric service is lost, the system automatically changes over to a battery. This battery is located inside the central control box and is constantly trickle-charged through the alarm system. The battery in this system will normally provide several days of protection and is even capable of sounding the alarm for a reasonable length of time.

With the new electrical regulations that require electric meters to be installed on the outside of a dwelling, all homes are susceptible to loss of electrical power from a burglar. All that the burglar has to do is to pull out the meter and it acts like a big switch, cutting off the entire power to the home. I don't recommend you use the meter to cut off your power, because it carries a lot of load current and when pulled out of its socket could cause a large electrical arc severely burning you. A burglar, though, might take this risk to disable your alarm system.

Delay Entry and Exit

I prefer a delay entry and exit feature that does not require the installation of a control station on the outside of your home. This control station is used to arm or disarm the alarm system when entering or leaving.

Outside control stations are subject to weather and provide another opportunity for the burglar to tamper with your alarm system. This tampering can be easily prevented but no method is foolproof.

Good systems provide for a variable delay entry and exit timing system to allow the owner to set the alarm system before he exits the home and to turn it off after he enters. This is done from a control station inside the home. This system prevents the triggering of the alarm for some preset period of time. The door may be opened and closed as many times as you wish until this time has expired. Several seconds after leaving the home, this door becomes part of the delay entry system. When the owner returns, another timing circuit times the period from when the same door is opened until the system is turned off. This delay entry and exit should only be used on the door that is usually used for entering and leaving the home. All other doors will cause an alarm to sound instantaneously when they are opened.

The time delay feature allows the owner to disarm the system with his key before the alarm is triggered. These timing circuits can be adjusted to allow up to several minutes but it is generally found that about forty-five seconds is sufficient to enter or exit.

I know that forty-five seconds seems short but just try this little experiment. Use your watch to time the number of seconds that it takes you to casually open your door and walk to a central location where the control station might be located. This station is normally located near the main entrance. Simulate taking your key out to disarm the system. You will be surprised that forty-five seconds is more than enough time.

Longer times can be used when necessary. It should be remembered that longer times give a burglar time to get into the home and try to disable the system. Good systems will include protection of the control station so that any attempt to remove the cover plate of the control station would cause the alarm to go off. So even if the burglar were to run into the home and attempt to remove the cover plate, his efforts would only trigger the alarm system, instead of disabling it.

Panic Systems

A panic system is a circuit that is constantly ready to trigger the alarm whether the system is turned on or not. Picture yourself working in the kitchen. You hear a noise on the back porch and see a complete stranger entering the back door. He is moving too quickly for you to run out the front door. What would you do? Of course, the best thing for you to do is to get out of the house as fast as possible, but that is not always an option.

With a panic system, push buttons are located in areas (kitchen, laundry room, basement, family rooms, bedrooms, next to front door) where you would normally spend your time. By pushing one of these buttons, the alarm system is triggered. This will happen whether or not the system is armed. It is a 24-hour-a-day guardian. Of course, you will have to teach your children not to play with them. This is not usually a problem because once they have tried this button the first time, so much noise occurs that everyone will know that they did it. They don't usually try it again.

The only way to turn off a panic trip, in most systems, is by operating a reset switch located in the central control box. This box is locked and normally hidden. The reason for this method of reset is that if an intruder were to try to force you to turn off the alarm after you triggered it, you could simply say that you can't. Although this might risk harm to you, you must decide which is the greater risk. If you turn it off is he going to harm you? I think that the intruder is the greater risk. Since he only has seconds to think of what to do about this wailing siren, he will more than likely flee.

Fire Protection

Fire is the greatest threat to life in the U.S. Any good alarm system will include a fire-detection system as part of the main control panel. All that you have to do to make use of it is to run some more wires and buy some smoke and heat detectors. I always recommend a smoke detector in the upper and lower hall with heat detectors in the basement (at least over the heater) and in the attic. You should check to see what the local zoning requirements state. This could affect the resale of your home in the future. Many townships are requiring that a home be equipped with smoke detectors before it can be sold.

Detectors used in the attic should be ones with a rating of 190° F. The reason for this is that attics reach a temperature of at least 140° F during the summer. This would be sufficient to trip the normal heat sensor used for the rest of the home.

System Status Indicator Lights

When the system is to be armed, it is necessary to know if all the windows and doors are closed. Better systems provide both a method of telling you at the control panel whether the system is ready to be armed and if the system is already armed. These lights are very helpful if someone leaves a window slightly opened. You could spend a lot of time trying to figure out what was wrong with the system without these lights. When you enter your home it is difficult to tell whether the system is armed or not unless there is a visual or audible indicator (sometimes referred to as a Sonalert or warning horn). Seeing a red light will tell you that the system is armed and that it must be disarmed before the entry delay has expired or the alarm will trip.

Some systems combine audible and visual indications. They have indicator lights and a small transistorized speaker that gives off a high-pitched sound to tell you the entry delay timer is running and that you have to disarm the system or the alarm will go off. These speakers are referred to by many names, such as entry warning horn, Sonalert or Mini-howler. They are often mounted in a wall switch plate or just about anywhere in proximity to the delayed entry door so that you will be sure to hear them. Wires from the central control send a signal to the warning device when the delay entry timer is triggered.

These are excellent to use to remind people that they have just tripped the alarm. People who are not familiar with your system find this helpful. You might say that this is a good alert for the burglar to tell him that he has a short time to defeat the alarm, but there are two reasons why this is of no concern. One reason is that the control station is protected by a "tamper switch" which will, if he trys to defeat it, trigger the alarm anyway. The second is that the burglar will normally be so surprised that he will, most times, simply leave quickly.

Lighting Control Circuits

A lighting control circuit can be of two types. One is simply a set of dry contacts that can be used like a switch on interior and exterior lights. The second is a set of output terminals that can be used to operate a low voltage relay, which will act as a switch to turn on interior and exterior lights. The second method is better because the contacts of the relay have a very high rating and can support the larger lighting loads that exterior spotlights represent. Most competent alarm supply stores can instruct you how this can be done.

Remember, when an alarm occurs you will want lights to go on inside and outside the home. This will make the burglar take off rather than hide. If he chooses to stay and hide, his location will be more easily revealed to the police if they have sufficient lighting to check out the home.

7 | What are the Types of Detecting Devices?

There are scads of devices on the market for detecting everything from glass breakage to pressure on a floor board. Many of these devices have uses that are necessary for the commercial or industrial field. Using devices like these in a residential situation would be a poor selection and create more problems than it would solve. I will describe a few of the more common types of devices, giving what I believe to be their advantages and disadvantages. I will also recommend whether they should be considered for residential installation.

Magnetic Contacts

These are the most common detecting devices and there are many varieties. They usually consist of two parts: a small reed switch that is hermetically sealed in a plastic case and a magnet that is also encased in plastic. These two units are designed to be used together. The switch portion is placed on the stationary object (e.g., door frame) and the magnet is mounted on the moving object (e.g., door). While the two units are in close proximity to each other (side by side), the magnet pulls the reed switch closed, allowing monitoring current from the alarm system to pass through. When the door is opened causing the magnet to move away from the switch, the reed springs open, breaking the circuit and causing an alarm to sound.

The advantages of these are that they are easily mounted and very reliable in operation. It is difficult to defeat this type of switch, but they must be mounted in such a way to prevent someone from unscrewing them from the object on which they are mounted or jumping the wires connecting the reed switch to defeat the system.

The major disadvantage is that unless they are of the recessed version, which is hidden from view, they are not very attractive. If surface mounted, you must be careful not to damage them when working around them or moving heavy objects near them. The tolerance for the distance between the reed switch and the magnet is sometimes critical. This depends a lot on the quality of the switch. If the switch uses a weak magnet, sometimes the warping of a window or door as the weather changes is enough to break the contact and set off an alarm. This can be overcome by using switches that have high "gap" ratings. If magnetic switches are used on metal doors or windows they should have a plastic separator (insulator) to prevent the magnet from being weakened by the metal of the frame.

Surface-mounted magnetic contacts are easily installed. The recessed version is more difficult because you must drill a hole for both the magnet and the switch portion and these holes must line up almost exactly or the switch won't work. Alarm suppliers have a small alignment tool that isn't very expensive and will assist you in aligning these holes. I recommend using recessed contacts wherever possible. They are difficult to see and do not spoil the appearance of your home.

If you are mounting recessed contacts on a window and don't have an aligning tool, simply drill the hole for the magnet first. Insert the magnet and place a tack on the end of the magnet. The magnet will hold the tack so that when you close the window the tack will make a hole that is the location to drill for the switch installation.

You must be careful to purchase the proper type of magnetic switch for your system. These switches come in two types — normally open and normally closed. If you install the wrong type your system won't work. Check with your equipment supplier. He will know which switch is used in your system.

Roller or Compression Contacts

Although many installers use roller or compression contacts, I have found them to be nothing but trouble. The roller switch uses a rolling ball that makes contact with a window or door as it closes. As the ball is depressed it breaks (or makes) the contact. When they get some dirt in them, however, they don't function properly. The push button or compression switch has a similar problem. The plunger when pushed in either makes or breaks a contact in the circuit. The problem here is also dirt. A little dirt can cause them to malfunction.

One thing we all know — dirt is going to get on anything used in a window or door frame. It's just the nature of the beast. I never use these contacts. They are cheaper and that is the only reason that I can see for an installer using them. Because of the type of operation, these contacts are more susceptible to malfunctioning due to door or window warping than are magnetic contacts. **I do not recommend** the use of roller or compression contacts in a residential system.

There is another type of roller contact that may be used in alarm systems and works well for the intended purpose. This type uses a roller on the end of a metal finger. The roller allows the finger to roll over irregular surfaces without getting hung up. These contacts are also used inside cash register drawers. Often one cash slot will have a roller switch installed. The money in this slot is never used unless there is a robbery. When all the money is taken out from under this switch, the alarm is triggered (normally a silent alarm).

Pull Traps

A pull trap is simply a switch that is activated by pulling out a pin or tab. There are several types. In one type there are two balls that oppose each other through spring tension. Wires from the alarm system are connected to each ball. There is an insulating tab inserted between the balls to prevent them from making contact. When this tab is pulled out, the balls come together and cause the alarm to sound.

A similar device uses two sets of balls, each with a tab between them. In this case, both the tabs and balls are metal. The cord connecting these tabs is a conductor. The purpose for this is to prevent someone from cutting the pull cord. If the cord is cut it will break the circuit causing an alarm.

Another type of pull trap has a spring-loaded contact so that if the pull cord is cut, the spring will trip the circuit. There are probably many more versions but by now you should have the idea.

Pull traps are excellent for protecting metal doors such as basement entrances that are all metal, or even a parked boat or motorcycle.

The major disadvantage is that the pull cord is easily spotted and the switches aren't very attractive. This limits their use to areas where beauty is not important (barns, garages, basements).

Metallic Tape

Metallic tape has been used for years on glass surfaces to detect breakage. Normally, when a pane of glass is smashed, the fractures in the glass will travel to the edges. Metallic tape is bonded to the surface of the glass by a lacquer coating so that the tape breaks when the glass breaks. This tape is actually a current-carrying conductor that is connected into the alarm system. When the tape is severed, the circuit is interrupted and the alarm system is triggered.

This is a relatively cheap method of protecting large glass surfaces against the more prevalent type of break-in, which is simply to break a pane of glass to gain access to the building. It does not prevent the professional burglar from cutting the glass carefully to avoid any breakage that would tear the tape.

Glass manufacturers have remedied this problem. They have manufactured glass with a plastic sheet embedded into it that prevents a section of the pane from being removed by cutting.

I do not recommend metallic tape for the normal residential installation because it is too ugly and difficult to connect into the alarm system without very obtrusive contact blocks mounted along the windowsills.

Glass Break Detectors

A glass break detector is a small detector that is usually mounted on a stationary type large window at the frame. A small sensor lies against the glass so that when the glass is broken it will trigger an alarm.

There is also a type of glass break detector that is mounted in the wall of a room in which the glass is to be protected. It detects the sound of breaking glass. The major drawback is that it must determine the difference between breaking glass and sounds that resemble breaking glass. This is a difficult task and can often lead to a high false-alarm rate. Many times when false alarms occur, the installer, in an attempt to solve the problem, will desensitize the detector to the point where it provides little, if any, protection.

I don't believe that it is necessary for the average owner to try to protect against glass breakage. This may be useful in stores where merchandise is just inside the window. The burglar will simply smash the glass, grab the item, and run.

In a residential alarm system the responsibility for detecting a forced entry should be left up to the door and window detectors. This policy agrees with the practice that we should require an actual entry before triggering an alarm. This policy alone will reduce significantly the number of false alarms that you will experience.

Statistics show that most forced entries occur through doors and windows. Rarely, though, does a burglar break out the glass and climb through the broken pane. Breaking the glass simply allows him to reach in and unlock the door or window.

Pressure Sensors and Mats

Pressure sensors are small devices used to detect the foot pressure of a burglar and either sound an alarm or allow a security force to determine his location. Some applications have been used in tiled entryways to alert the guard force or to trigger video cameras. These are rarely used in a residential system because they inhibit the use of the residence. You could not walk into areas using pressure sensors without triggering the alarm.

Mats are a type of pressure sensor made into a carpet-like mat. They can usually be cut to length and connected into an alarm system to detect the foot pressure of a burglar in a given area. They are made extremely thin to allow placement under carpeting without any noticeable bulge.

The major drawback of mats is that they do require concealment under carpets to be effective, and they cannot accept any direct weight from furniture or pets without triggering an alarm. They make an excellent backup system to be used in an interior zone of an alarm system if placed in an area that the burglar is very likely to enter (e.g., main hall, in front of a valuable item — portable T.V., silver set, or painting). After completing a successful entry into the house, the burglar isn't likely to realize that there is a backup system within the house that will set off the alarm. **I do not recommend** the use of mats in the primary zone of a residential alarm system unless they are to be used in an area where members of the household are extremely unlikely to enter after the alarm has been set. Remember, you do want to use the system when you are at home, but you don't want the system to limit the use of your home. Any limitation must be acceptable. If the mat prevents you from entering the basement this might be acceptable, but preventing you from using your family room would certainly not be acceptable.

Using mats in areas that produce constant false alarms would cause your neighbors to tire quickly of your alarm system. You would experience the "cry wolf syndrome."

Infrared Beams

Infrared beams are another "active system" like mats and sonic detectors. They require that you do not enter the area they are protecting. The method of operation is quite simple. There is a transmitter that when mounted on a fixed object (usually a wall), will transmit an infrared light beam to a receiver. Infrared light is used because the human eye cannot see this light frequency, therefore the beam is invisible. As long as the beam remains uninterrupted, the system will not trigger an alarm. When something comes between the transmitter and the receiver, the beam will be interrupted and an alarm will sound. Some systems have the transmitter and the receiver in the same unit and use mirrors to reflect the beam back to the receiver portion of the unit.

The advantage of an infrared system is that it requires little installation to protect a rather large area. It is not easily detected, since many of these transmitters are disguised to look like standard wall receptacles.

There are also some disadvantages. Infrared systems are slightly more expensive in some applications than other types of protective devices. They are an active device, so they should not be used in areas where your family or pets might enter accidentally, causing a false alarm. These systems are not normally used outside the home because animals, branches from trees, pieces of paper blown by the wind, and other moving objects can cause a false alarm. In the home they tend to inhibit the placement of furniture. After all, you could not forget about the infrared beam and place a chair in the way of the beam. The path must be completely unobstructed. Again, infrared makes an excellent system to be used in a second zone (interior zone) of a home if it is placed properly.

Photoelectric Beams

Photoelectric beams are similar to infrared beams except they use visible light. It has all the advantages of the infrared system and all the same disadvantages with one addition. It should not be used in an area for nighttime protection because it can be seen by the intruder and all that he has to do is to step over it. These are more commonly used in doorways of commercial establishments to monitor the entry or exit of people. **I do not recommend** the use of these at all in a residential alarm system.

Dialers

Some alarm systems use a device called a dialer. Dialers are normally mechanical devices that use a tape player with a direct connection to your commercial telephone line. In the event of a forced entry, the central processor of the alarm system initiates the dialer and also sounds a local alarm, except in those systems designed as silent alarm systems. The dialer can be programmed to dial the telephone number of the police station. When the police answer, the dialer will play a prerecorded message that usually states there is a burglary in progress at the following address and requests that the police respond.

The better designed systems will re-try the telephone number until it is answered in case the number is busy. The more expensive systems can be programmed to dial several numbers and give the same message. It is also possible to get a dual tape system that will dial the police for a forced entry that is triggered by the burglar alarm or dial the fire department for a fire triggered by the fire detection system.

I strongly recommend that if a dialer is used, an item called a "line capture device" be installed. This device prevents someone from interrupting the dialer by simply taking an extension phone off the hook immediately after entering your home.

There are many advantages to a dialer system. People with residences in very remote locations, such as farms or recreational areas where a local alarm might go unreported, could use a dialer which would call the police directly. This does not exclude the use of that loud audible alarm. I still believe that it is necessary to make lot of loud noise both internally and externally. You still want the burglar to know that his presence has been detected. The loud noise will, more often than not, frighten him off before he has time to find your valuables or do extensive damage to your home, but the noise combined with a dialer would be more protection.

In a situation where you do not wish to let the burglar know that an alarm system has been activated the dialer would work well. An example would be in a bank where the teller triggers an alarm when a holdup occurs. If the robbers hear the alarm they might injure someone or escape cleanly. Again **I do not recommend** using this system in an attempt to capture the burglar who has entered your house. Making as much noise as possible and turning on lights still provides the greatest protection against loss or injury. The dialer coupled with a system that accomplishes these goals is an excellent system.

The only real disadvantage of a dialer is that the average dialer can add from $150 to $300 to your system's cost. Since this cost is a one-time expenditure, you may still wish to install it.

Generally, when the dialer is purchased, the manufacturer allows one recording of the original taped message in the purchase price. Changes after this initial programming can be made but they will cost additional money. These changes can be done by either the manufacturer or a good local alarm dealer. It is possible to purchase a dialer with a built-in recording capability, but for the number of times that you might have to redo a tape this additional cost can't be justified. Another thing that might be considered a disadvantage by some is that if you have a false alarm, you must answer the police when they telephone to see if it is a false alarm or a real one. The normal practice of a police department is to call the residence to see if it is a real alarm before dispatching a patrol car. Some localities have even passed a law that requires the payment of a fine for a false alarm. The purpose of this fine is to discourage cheap systems that would keep the police busy answering false alarms all day.

8 | Should I or a Professional Install an Alarm System?

The answer to this question is no different than whether you should train your own dog or repair your own car. It depends on how much talent you have and even more, how much you are willing to learn. It is my personal feeling that it doesn't take enormous talent to install an alarm system. The system could easily cost from $1500 to $2500 depending on what you try to accomplish and who does the installation.

The first thing you must decide is what type of system you want to own. In Chapter 4, the advantages and disadvantages of each type of system were outlined. The modular systems need very little installation and require very little technical knowledge. The hard-wired system does require some knowledge about soldering and basic wiring techniques. I prefer the hard-wired system because of the degree of protection it offers and its dependability. If you have examined your home carefully and done a simple drawing showing the points that you wish to monitor, you will have some idea of the type of system necessary to do the job. If you see that you have one main hall that every room must use to have access to every other room, and there is no possible entry from the second floor or basement, maybe the modular system is perfect for you.

Let me try to give you some basic steps in making this decision.

1. Make a basic sketch of your home.
2. In this sketch, mark which doors and windows provide the most logical entry points for burglary. (It might not be necessary to

protect a very small window ten feet off the ground with no way
to get to it except with a ladder.)
3. Now, think like a burglar. Which path would you most likely take
as you went through the house? Keep in mind that we are protecting against the hit-and-miss burglar. These people are commonly interested in stereos, portable color T.V.s, money, guns,
jewelry.
4. See if these paths converge in one central area (e.g., main hall,
stairway).

      Now that you have done this you should have some
idea whether you can use a system that must just protect one main
area or several detached areas of the house.

Modular Systems

      The modular system is the simplest to install. These
systems are commonly self-contained. They are generally motion
detectors and use a beam to detect movement. In most instances all
that they need is an A.C. outlet. If you have one main hall or central
room, select a location for this system so that the beam can reach
the largest possible area. The unfortunate problem is that often the
best location for this system is where there is no table or shelf on
which it can sit. If it is possible, place a small table or shelf at this
location. If not, you'll have to select another location and reduce the
optimum performance of the system.
      It is necessary to have an A.C. outlet in the same area
as the shelf or table. Follow the system directions carefully. Don't
make the assumption that you know better than the system de-
signers. Do what they tell you or you will more than likely have
problems.
      Now to test the system. Don't do crazy things like
crawl along the baseboard or climb over the top of a set of book-
shelves. Although most systems will detect this anyway, it isn't necessary. You know what type of system you have and where it's located. The average burglar wouldn't have this knowledge. Enter the
area and see if the system alarms. The next test is the toughest —
the operational test. Place it in service and see what happens over
time.
      Please be prepared for a false alarm. Even with pro-
fessionally installed alarm systems there is a small possibility of a
false alarm in the initial stages of operational testing. There may be

some bugs that need working out. If you get an alarm the first night you use the thing, you can almost be assured that it is false. I would still take the precautions that I have outlined in Chapter 12.

Hard-Wired Systems

It would be absolutely foolish of me to try to include in this book enough in-depth instructions to take you step-by-step through the installation of a hard-wired system. Instead, I will tell you that alarm equipment dealers have instruction manuals that clearly show every step in the installation of a hard-wired system and all its associated components.

If you install the system a section at a time, you will be able to reduce the impact on your budget by spreading the cost of the required materials over a longer time. You will also be dealing with one type of detection device at a time (e.g., magnetic contacts) and the dealer will be able to help you resolve whatever problems you might have with that particular part of the installation. The key to a successful installation is to work slowly. Don't allow yourself to get overtired to the point where you make careless mistakes. Neatly solder and tape all connections. Make drawings that you understand to tell you where you ran a certain wire and what is in which circuit.

Most good central control panels come equipped with all the features I have listed in Chapter 6. It's not necessary to make use of every feature from the start. There are certain features that you can come back later and install. I just find that if you don't install everything you want from the beginning, you probably won't ever get to it.

After a circuit is installed, test it out with an ohm meter or a bell. These are simple circuits. There isn't anything really complicated about them. If you do run into a problem, stop. Don't go on and complicate the thing to the point where no one can figure out what you have done. Go to the dealer, bring your drawings, and ask him what has happened. He has seen just about every problem and can usually tell you how to figure it out.

The most frequent mistake is to believe your control panel isn't functioning when it is actually something that you have done. In all the systems I have installed, I have only had one defective control panel. The supplier replaced it on the spot and the system was in operation that day.

Installation of a hard-wired system can be done by one professional but it is difficult. It takes two people to install a hard-wired system. There is simply no way that you can be on both ends of a wire at the same time when that wire goes through a wall. Always be patient with your helper. He or she would like to finish the system, too. It's not their desire to frustrate you. So if you set reasonable goals, you will still have a friend, wife, or husband when the job is finished.

I know when you see the materials involved in a hard-wired system you will think that this is more than you can handle. Just remember that once you have done this job you will never have to do it again.

In the beginning of this chapter, I stated that a good system could cost from $1500 to $2500 depending on who installed it. This system installed by you would most likely cost less than $500. This is a substantial savings to you and should be an incentive.

System Maintenance

How to maintain your system is certainly one of the easiest questions to answer. Since most systems today are electronic, the failure rate is extremely low. They either work well from the first time they are energized or they will fail in the first few days of operation (only a very small percentage fail).

The modular system usually has a warranty that allows you to return the system to the manufacturer for repair. For this reason I recommend saving the box and packing materials. It makes it much easier to ship the equipment back if needed.

Hard-wired systems also have warranties. You must be careful that the warranty doesn't state "invalid, unless installed by a professional installer." I have found that even where the warranty states this the companies are willing to make repairs. This is assuming you haven't altered the control panel which could invalidate any warranty.

In a hard-wired system the entire central control processor, the "brain" if you like, comes inside a sturdy steel box. This panel is usually easily taken off by removing a few small screws holding the panel in the box. It is not necessary to take the mounted box off the wall and return the entire thing. If you have taken the time to carefully tag each wire in the control box, all that you have to do is unfasten the wires and let them hang down. When the new panel arrives, put each wire back on the tagged terminal number. Be sure that the screws are tightened.

The manufacturer knows that your system is out of order and will make every effort to get it back in service as soon as possible. I recommend that you first contact the supplier who sold you the equipment. Often he will see that the panel is defective and give you an immediate replacement, returning the panel for repair himself.

If your system has been installed by a professional and you have taken the time to check out his credentials, as I recommended, all that is necessary is to call him. They will normally be there the same day if possible and will handle any warranty problems.

If your system is one that uses central office guards or control systems, the company will send someone quickly. You pay a premium for such systems and they should provide better-than-average service. If they give you any runaround, I suggest that you consider renting your equipment from another agency. I believe you will find that the industry leaders will give you excellent service. Their reputation depends on it.

In a system that you have installed, the most you will have to do is to replace the storage battery. It is difficult for me to say how often to do this. Some batteries have a one-year life while others have a five-year life. What **I do recommend** is that you mark on your calendar on the same dates twice each year "check alarm system." On those dates all that is necessary is to remove the source of A.C. power from your alarm system.

This can be done in two ways. One is to simply unplug the small trickle-charged transformer in the wall or unscrew the leads marked A.C. on the panel terminal board, whichever is easier. After you have removed the A.C. supply, the system should automatically throw over to the battery system. If you don't have indicating lights, your battery is definitely bad (or your charging system is defective — this is rare) and must be replaced. Simply unplug the connectors and install a new one. If your system still has indicator lights after removing the A.C. source, you still will not know whether the battery is good. The reason is that there is often enough "surface charge" on even a bad battery to operate these lights because of their low current drain. The real acid test is to arm the system and open a window or door to trip the system. If the battery fails to sound the siren or bell, replace it. If it sounds the siren or bell it is still good.

I recommend an even safer method of insuring that your battery doesn't fail. Replace it every year on the same date whether it needs it or not. It is not very expensive and this is cheap insurance against a failure. Even if the method of replacing the battery once a year is used, you should still check the system functions as described above at the half-year point.

As I said, there isn't really much maintenance that is necessary and it's something you can easily do. The real problem is to remember to check the battery backup system twice each year. If you forget, you can bet that when you need the battery backup system, it will fail to function.

9 | Where Can Alarm Equipment Be Purchased?

My first advice would be to stay away from the chain stores and department stores. Too often, their sales people are just that — sales people. They are there to sell you the product and they rarely have any in-depth knowledge about the equipment. You must be able to count on their experience to answer any questions that you might have about operation or installation problems. If you deal with a chain store they will most likely refer you back to the manufacturer, and you will be trying to resolve your problem by mail.

The yellow pages of your telephone book often list equipment dealers who not only install alarm equipment but sell it to "do-it-yourself" installers. These people generally know their product and are willing to work with you to help you with any problem that might arise. By simply telephoning a supplier and explaining what your desires are you will be able to tell if he is willing to help you with your installation if you get into trouble. Some suppliers will tell you right up front that they will sell only to certified alarm installers. You should be able to find someone in your area who will be helpful.

If it appears that no one is available, write to one of the major manufacturers of alarm equipment (see Manufacturers, p. 145) and ask them if they can help. They know the distributors in their areas and will know who would be helpful.

You should also avoid the problem of shopping for price alone. An alarm system is one purchase where you get what you pay for. Don't expect to get a top-line piece of alarm equipment and pay basement prices. There will be a strong temptation to buy from a chain store or maybe even from an ad on T.V. These ads all claim that their system needs no installation and will protect your entire house. Don't believe it. The units are cheap and require no installation, but they also give very little protection.

Since the installation of an alarm system in your house is probably a one-time event, it is time to spend the money necessary to get a quality system that will be reliable and free of false-alarm problems.

Since it might be time for some words of encouragement, I'll tell you what just happened. While I was writing this chapter, a friend of mine called. I had assisted him in the installation of a hard-wired system for his parents' house about five years ago. At the time, his father thought that the entire idea was ridiculous. My friend called to tell me that while he and his family had stepped out of the house for just forty minutes someone kicked in his back door. The system turned on the lights and made lots of racket. Apparently it was enough to scare off the burglar. The police were called by a neighbor and were in the house when my friend returned home. Nothing was lost and the only damage was to the back door.

If you are wondering whether he had decals on the doors and windows — he did. Apparently this burglar didn't believe them.

It is difficult to prove to someone the value of an alarm system. You will never know whether your system scared a burglar away unless he leaves some form of physical evidence. My friend's father didn't believe in alarm systems either.

So when looking for your alarm equipment, I suggest that you exercise great care in selecting the equipment dealer. Do it in much the same way that you would select any other dealer. You'll know what type of help he is going to be from the very start by the way that he answers your questions.

A Professionally Installed Alarm System — Getting Bids

The best way to get a good price or at least a fair price on an alarm system installation is through competitive bidding. You must create the competitive atmosphere.

First, you must know exactly what you want done. You should be able to state that you want exterior protection on all doors and windows, a panic circuit and where you want the buttons, fire and smoke detection, delay entry and exit. Some options are sure to surface that you haven't considered. To avoid being put into a position of comparing apples and oranges, have each estimator list the option and associated cost separately. This will allow you to compare the system's base price and then give separate consideration to any additional options.

The key to a successful bidders' meeting is to make sure that you have at least three companies bidding and make sure that their estimators are all at your home at the same time. That's right — at the same time. When one bidder sees that his competition is there, you will be sure that the bids will be reasonably low to start. Take all of them through the house together and try to avoid leaving them alone for private discussions.

All bids should be written with every item spelled out clearly. It is better to ask for the written estimate right then rather than have them mail it to you. I would recommend you choose the bidder that elects to use equipment which is an industry standard, not some off-brand. If you don't recognize the manufacturer, ask if he has some literature that he can leave with you. Go to the library and use the Thomas Registers. These books list every manufacturer in the U.S. They will tell you the size of the company and the parent company if there is one. Avoid a company that is small and has only been in business for a few years.

Ask each bidder if he would be willing to give you a few names of people in the area where he has installed systems. This will allow you to call these people and see if they have been satisfied with the installation and service. If the bidders refuse to give you any names and try to tell you that they are private, tell them that you won't consider them for bid.

When you call these references tell them exactly why you are calling and don't ask them any particulars about their systems' functions. The only things that you need to know are:

1. Was the installation neat and done on time?
2. Were there any false alarms? If so, how often and was the company able to remedy the problem?
3. Did the company respond in a reasonable time to calls for service?
4. Has any of their equipment failed since it was installed?
5. If they were to have a system installed again, is there anything they would do differently?

You will find that most people will not mind answering these questions. I would also check with the Better Business Bureau to see if there were any complaints about the company.

This doesn't ensure that there were no dissatisfied customers. All it says is that they apparently weren't angry enough to file a complaint. If any of this information checks out badly don't consider that company as a bidder.

It's not proper to ask the people that you call about cost so I wouldn't even try. Most people, after they find out why you are asking these questions and who you are, will be willing to help. You must be willing to tell them who you are and where you live so that they know you are a neighbor. If they refuse to answer your questions on the telephone, ask if you might stop over and meet them.

Now for some words of encouragement. On one system where this procedure was not followed the bids ranged from $1700 to $2400. When the sister of this person used the described bidding procedure the bids for exactly the same system ranged from $1250 to $1400. Quite a savings!

Sometimes bidders will attempt to confuse you with terminology. If this happens, ask them to explain how a particular item functions. If you still don't understand, ask one of the other bidders present if he could explain it more clearly.

Check the following items carefully:

1. Make sure that each estimator designates in writing what equipment he intends to install and its intended locations.
2. Make sure that the contract states who is responsible for any damage done to the home during installation and that this damage must be repaired to the owner's satisfaction. If these items aren't in the contract it is perfectly correct to write them into it. Just make sure that it is on both copies and that he signs his initials and the date beside each addition.
3. If you have any questions about the wording in the contract ask him to leave the contract with you and show it to a lawyer before signing it.
4. Be sure there is a completion date in the contract.
5. Never, never pay the entire amount of the contract before the system is completed and working. **I recommend** not paying more than half down and the rest to be paid on completion of the installation. Agree to mail the finished payment within ten working days of the completion of the installation. At least this will give you some time to get them back if there is some malfunction.
6. If they have to return to repair some item after the final date of installation, prepare a brief note (in duplicate) and have them

sign it. This note should simply recognize the fact that they were at your home to repair (let them fill in the item) on that date. This could be of assistance if you have to take them to court later for a bad or incomplete job.

7. If they refuse to comply with your wishes, don't do business with them. They can be the most polite people in the world, but if they refuse to do business in a manner that will insure your satisfaction with the job, then you don't want to do business with them.

8. If there are any warranties on the equipment — usually there are warranties on the central control panel — or on the installation, ask for them in writing before the contract is signed. Don't believe this, "Don't worry, lady. If you have any problems in the first five years just pick up the phone and we will come right out and repair it." Verbal contracts, although often held as legal, are difficult to prove.

9. See if you can get him to agree to a number for excessive false alarms in a given period. Have the contract state that he agrees to replace the item or entire system at his cost if the false alarms exceed "?" number in the first three months. I would consider one false alarm a month excessive, but you might want to give him a break and allow him a couple in the first week. After all, there may be some bugs in the system that they have to work out. If he refuses, ask him if he lacks faith in his equipment or installers. This usually works.

10. Check with the local police to see if they have any objections to this installer. Often, if they have had a number of false alarms from equipment installed by a certain company, they aren't afraid to say so.

If you take the time to do all these steps, you won't be one of the large number of people each year who have a system installed by a fly-by-night company just to have so many problems with it that they have to disable the system in order to live in their home. A well-installed system, using name-brand equipment, should be able to function for more than ten years with no problems.

If you fail to follow the steps that I've outlined, you will find that there are virtually no companies that are willing to come and clean up some other installer's mess. I have often been called by someone recommended to me by a friend because his system wasn't working and he couldn't get his installer to repair it. I hated to go in and try to cure these problems. In the time it took me to figure out what this person had done wrong, I could have installed an entire system and made much more money. That's why most companies will only agree to install a completely new system. If they said they would have to charge you $1500 to straighten out the system you'd tell them that you could get a new one installed for that much money and you'd be right.

A word to the wise. Take the time in the beginning and you will have a lot fewer headaches in the end. There are mostly reputable installers out there. But if you don't take the proper steps you will probably find the one who's not reputable.

Maintenance Contracts

For those systems that are installed by you, there is no maintenance contract. After all, you installed it so you are responsible for the maintenance — what little there is. What about those systems that are installed by professional contractors? Their service contracts are not much different than a contract on your T.V. There is one major difference. Alarm systems need very little maintenance.

Most professional contractors offer a monthly contract that includes checking the system once a year and responding to any service calls resulting from false alarms or failed equipment. If you have followed my instructions on obtaining the best price for your system, the false-alarm problems should be nonexistent. So, all there is left is the failure of a piece of equipment.

Since the failure rate of this type of equipment is so low, simply call the installer if and when you have a problem and pay him whatever his rate is to fix it. The only exception to this recommendation is for the central station systems that are sold through large commercial companies. These systems usually require that you pay a monthly service fee and maintenance is part of that fee. In this case you don't really have an option.

Most of the equipment you purchase, if you install your own system, comes separately warranteed. In case of a failure, you must contact the manufacturer. I have found them to be most cooperative. They will usually ship you a replacement component upon receiving your failed component. Be sure to keep the copies of your purchase receipts so that you can verify the date of purchase. Send a photocopy of this receipt along with the failed component — always keep the original. If the failed component is the control panel itself, you should telephone the manufacturer and explain your situation. They will usually send you a replacement panel immediately and allow you to return your panel at the same time. This is to insure that you will have your system out of service a minimum of time.

You must have any warranty in writing in order for it to be enforceable. The verbal promise of an installer is not sufficient. All warranties must be in writing and dated.

As for service contracts, **I recommend** that you save your money.

10 | Is There a Low-Budget Alarm System?

Please don't be offended by the description of this system. There are many people who simply can't afford to purchase an alarm system which might cost several hundred dollars but who, unfortunately, live in a high crime area. For those people I have developed a simple design for an alarm system that would give protection while a person is home and would cost less than $5 per door or window. It could be built in pieces so that each $5 invested represents another door or window protected.

This alarm is not very attractive but it will work at least as well as the common smoke detectors used in most homes today. The parts are easy to purchase from a major electronics store. Simply take along the directions and the drawings to the store. Most people who work in this type of store will be glad to help. If you feel that building this system is more than your talents will allow, there are cheap, small portable alarms that you could purchase one at a time. Many of these alarms cost around $10. You will probably find that most other designs, although more attractive, do not make nearly as much noise as the design presented here.

How It Works

If you will please refer to Diagram 1 on page 65, I will try to trace the operation. String "A" would normally be attached to the door or window you wish to alarm. Opening the door or window will pull the string that is attached to the popsicle stick "B." The stick will be pulled out from between the jaws of the clothespin and the tacks on the inner side of the jaws will snap together. Electricity from the battery will flow from one side of the battery through one tack to the other tack. From here it goes through the wire to the buzzer and causes an alarm. To silence the alarm, the popsicle stick must be inserted between the jaws of the clothespin again. Simple but effective.

Construction

Begin by cutting a piece of wood that measures about 5" x 5". Be sure it is about ½" thick. This is the base for the alarm. Mount the buzzer in the upper left-hand corner of the wood (see Diagram 1 for layout). This can be accomplished by use of a strong tape such as silver duct tape commonly used by air-conditioning and heating installers. It can be found in most hardware stores. Place the tape around the buzzer and around the board. Be sure to remember to cut the tape away from the hole in the center of the buzzer. This hole is the diaphragm of the buzzer and makes the sound. If you were to leave tape covering it, the sound would be severely reduced.

Wrap the white wire from the buzzer around the point of a thumbtack. If you find that this wire is very short you can make it longer by taking a wire wrap (twist-tie) from a loaf of bread and stripping the plastic coating from the end abou:t ½" back. Wrap one end of this wire wrap around the white wire and the other around the tack.

After this, press the tack into the inside jaw of the clothespin. It may be necessary to drill a small hole through the jaws of the clothespin so that when you press in the tack, the wood of the clothespin doesn't split. Drill through both jaws of the clothespin at once because you will have to press a tack in each jaw. It is these two tacks that make the contacts for the alarm. Be sure to use tacks that do not have a plastic or rubber coating. (See Diagram 2.)

Now you must mount the battery holder in the upper right-hand corner of the block of wood, across from the buzzer. Two small screws can be used for this purpose. It's not necessary to drill holes through the plastic holder because they are already provided.

Now take the black wire from the battery holder and strip off about ½" of the insulation from the end. Tape this bare end of the wire against the side of the metal case of the buzzer. We would normally connect this wire to one of the wires from the buzzer, but you will notice that there is only one wire provided by the manufacturer. That is because he assumes you will be mounting this buzzer in a metal case and that the case of the buzzer can act as the second wire. So, taping the black wire to the side of the buzzer was exactly the same as connecting it to one of the wires in the buzzer.

Diagram 1

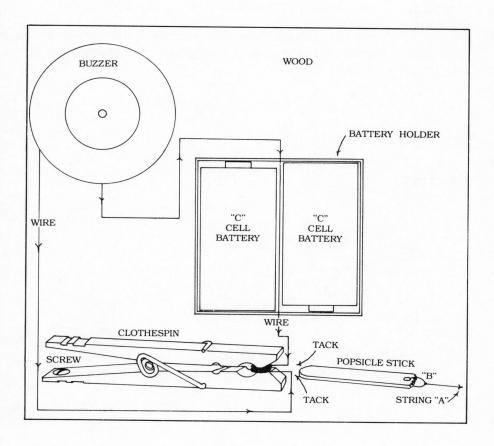

The red wire from the battery holder should be wrapped around the point of the second tack after stripping off ½" of insulation. This tack is pressed into the inside of the other jaw of the clothespin.

The wiring is now complete. If you insert the batteries following the outline in the inside bottom of the battery holder, the alarm should ring. To stop it from sounding, you must insert the popsicle stick between the jaws of the clothespin. The clothespin is wood and therefore an insulator. It prevents the current from flowing from one tack to the other.

The clothespin should be screwed down to the wood block in the position shown in Diagram 1. This can be done by drilling another hole in one of the flat spots on the back of the clothespin where it is squeezed. Put the screw through this hole and screw it down to the block.

It might be easier to attach a string to the popsicle by making a hole in the end of the stick and tying the string through the hole (see Diagram 1).

Diagram 2

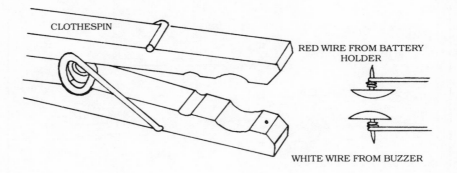

Setting the Trap

Setting the trap is a rather simple matter. All that you must do is decide which door or window you wish to protect. Let's say that you want to protect the front door. Simply lay the alarm on the floor to the side of the door opening. Tie a toothpick to the other end of the string (see Diagram 1 — String "A"). This toothpick will prevent the string from pulling out from under the tape that you will use to attach it to the door.

Tape the string to the door near the edge. When the door is opened the string will pull out the popsicle stick and set off the alarm.

You might think that this alarm wouldn't wake you out of a sound sleep but it is much louder than some of the commercial smoke detectors which are supposed to wake you in case of fire. In the middle of the night this will sound especially loud. It costs less than $5 to build. If you want to save additional money, some electronics chain stores offer a battery free simply by asking for a battery card. This card entitles you to a free battery every month. Check your area for stores that offer a similar service.

If you really cannot afford to buy a great system, why not build one of these a month until all major doors and windows are alarmed? They might warn you of a break-in in the middle of the night and possibly save your life.

The Low-Budget Alarm System Parts List

1 — 5" x 5" x ½" piece of wood (scrap will do)
1 — wooden clothespin (spring-clip type)
2 — plain metal thumbtacks
1 — wire wrap (twist-tie)
3 — small wood screws or sheet metal screws
1 — wooden popsicle stick
2 — "D" cell batteries
1 — "D" cell battery holder
1 — 1.5 volt D.C. buzzer. This size (1.5v D.C.) is important.

---

11 | How Well Should I Hide My Alarm System?

It is certainly true that part of the advantage of an alarm system is the element of surprise a burglar experiences when he attempts to break into your home. I simply debate whether the surprise must come from the fact that there were no decals or signs warning the intruder that a system was in use or the ability of the system to detect the intruder. This argument about whether to warn an intruder with decals will rage on forever. You must decide for yourself. I will present my arguments in Chapter 13.

There are basically three parts of the system that should be considered for concealment.

First there is the arming station. The only time that I believe it is necessary to conceal this station is if you are foolish enough to use a push button type arming switch inside the home instead of a key-type switch. Some people say that it is easier to have a simple push button inside the home to arm the system. I don't believe that it is any major inconvenience to have to use a key. The key at least prevents a burglar from simply disarming the system by pushing a button if he has managed to get by your perimeter protection. If you use a keyed station inside the home it can be anywhere that is convenient — usually in the main hall near the primary entrance.

There is an advantage to having a keyed station in plain sight and a disadvantage. The advantage is that if a burglar looks into the home and sees the system's red light is on, he knows the system is armed and he might get caught. The disadvantage is that if he looks inside and the system's green light is on he knows you forgot to arm the system and it's safe for him to break in. Since most burglaries occur when you are away from home or asleep, I don't think that this is a real disadvantage.

The second item is detection devices. They should be concealed as well as possible. Some of these devices lose their effectiveness if they can be easily seen. Contacts may be recessed into the wood framing of the doors or windows that they are monitoring. Where this isn't possible don't be concerned. The burglar must still defeat the contact if he sees it and that's no easy task.

Devices like infrared and sonic detectors should also be concealed as well as possible. If they can be seen they can be avoided. The ultrasonic transmitters are very difficult to approach unless you provide a shielded approach like an adjacent wall. You should look at these devices and try to determine if they can be approached without the device being alarmed. If they can, the installation should be changed to solve this problem.

Mats are only effective if they are placed under carpets in such a way that they cannot be seen. When a mat is installed it should be done in such a way that the thief will have to step on it, not in a way that he might step on it. That's why many installers place them at the top of steps or on the first three or four steps from the landing. It's very difficult to jump over a mat from the top landing to the fourth step without it.

Third is the central processor panel. The central processor is installed inside a closet out of plain sight. This is the heart of the system. If installed properly it is very difficult for a burglar to get into this box. Its location is essential to the installation of the system since all of the wires start from and return to it. There is no real need to worry about the central control box, however, because by the time a burglar gets into the home and anywhere near this location your system should have done its job. He should be on his way out the door.

If you disagree with me and believe that it is easier to have a simple push button to arm the system from inside the home, at least have the sense to conceal it well. A good location for it is inside a closet on the side of the door frame to the left or right. There is usually a small section of wall available. Rarely does anyone open a closet and look around the door frame to see if anything is on that section of wall.

As you can see, most of these points are opinions and are open to discussion and disagreement. These are my experienced opinions. You are welcome to do as you please. My feeling is that you are trying to protect against the majority of burglars who are non-professionals. You are trying to accomplish this with a system that will cost as little as possible while being as simple and free from false alarms as possible. The systems I have described in this book have functioned well for many years with so few problems that you could say they were trouble free.

Disclosing Information About Your Alarm System

In the military, there are many things that are classified "secret." The way that the military prevents everyone from knowing every secret is fairly simple. If you don't absolutely need to know a certain thing that is classified secret, in order to perform your work, then you aren't allowed to see it. This practice is called "need to know." It works very well.

This restriction applies to every rank from private to general. If the commanding officer of a base wants to know something that has nothing to do with the performance of his duties, the security officer will deny him access to this information.

The purpose for this practice is to limit the amount of information that any one person has. If you don't know anything about a secret, it's very difficult to tell it to someone else. In the case of your alarm system, there is a very strong temptation to brag about its capabilities. This is a type of "can you top this?" game. Whenever you reveal something about your alarm system it weakens your system. The reason is the person you told now has information that he really didn't need to know and can now, therefore, reveal it to someone else.

I'm sure you are thinking, "Well certainly I can trust my own brother!" **My recommendation** in this case is to tell your brother that the system works well, but that you don't really understand all the electronics of it. To you this seems like I'm saying not to trust your brother. That's not it at all. I don't expect your brother to burglarize your home. He might, without thinking that he is doing something wrong, get into a conversation with a friend and in trying to add his knowledge, tell that friend about all the fine features that his brother's alarm system has. All the time this friend or maybe his younger brother in another room is listening. Maybe they will learn something that will allow them to defeat your system. The problem with a secret is once you have told someone it is no longer a secret. The information you tell to someone in the strictest confidence might end up being repeated many times. Do your friends a favor and don't tell them something you want kept a secret.

Now what about the police? In most cases it makes little difference to the police whether you have an alarm system. Most police departments do not maintain any records on this information. It is extremely unlikely information such as this will ever get passed on to each officer on patrol or to succeeding administrations. It is more important to have a system that turns itself off after a period of time. If you are away when the system is sounding, the police will investigate. However, if after some reasonable period of time the system keeps ringing, the police must make some effort to restore peace to the neighborhood. They might do severe damage to your system, your home, or both in an attempt to silence this disturbance.

What about babysitters? All they really need to know is where you will be and what not to touch such as the panic switches. You can tell them if the system were to go off it will reset in twenty minutes or whatever time you have set it for.

Of course, if you are going to have someone in your home for some extended period of time, they will have to be told certain things about the alarm. These items should be:

1. What doors and windows have to be closed before you can arm your alarm system.
2. If your system uses infrared or mats, you must tell them what areas to avoid. You should show them the "line-of-sight" for the infrared beams so they do not interrupt the beam by placing something like a chair in the beam path.
3. If your system restricts pet movement, you must tell your guests where to put the pets when going out or arming the system.
4. Tell them the length of time the system will sound if it is triggered.
5. Show them how to reset the system for a normal trip and for fire or panic alarm.
6. Give them a key.

What not to tell someone. It's not necessary to tell anyone about the second zone features since they are only used when you are away on vacation. During these times there is no one in your home anyway.

In summary, tell as little as possible to as few people as possible.

12 | What Should I Do When My Alarm System Goes Off?

This section might seem a bit unnecessary. Of course we all know what to do when our alarm system goes off. Or do we?

First it depends on when the system goes off. If you are not in the house, your neighbors will normally report it to the police who will respond and make a check of the premises to determine the cause of the alarm. This is why the self-timing feature is so important. You don't want the alarm to sound twenty-four hours a day for two weeks while you are on vacation.

If you are home alone, not in bed but in the normal living area of the house, you will have to make some check of the house if only to satisfy your own pounding heart. **I recommend** that you first check the front door. If it is secure, open it and *get out of there.* Don't stop to get your purse, the cat, or whatever. Just get out! Go to the nearest neighbor. Call the police and wait for them. When they arrive, ask them to check out the premises.

If there is some reason that you cannot leave, like children in bed, *get your children into a front bedroom and lock the door.* Turn on the lights. Open the front window and yell as loud as possible. Yell a neighbor's name so that someone will not think that kids are playing pranks. When the police arrive, tell them to check the premises. If a neighbor arrives, discourage him from doing the job of the police. Ask him to call the police if you could not. Then ask him to remain in plain sight until the police arrive.

If you happen to have your keys with you, drop them to the police. I suggest that you always take your keys into your bedroom with you. If you leave them in plain sight, someone entering your home could use them to turn off your alarm system. Do not get your gun and attempt to find the burglar!

If you disagree with me and you still think it is wiser to search for the intruder, try this experiment. Turn off all the lights in your house and try to find someone. Now imagine what it would be like if you awoke from a sound sleep and the burglar was armed. You will find that there are numerous places that someone could hide in your home.

A burglar will normally attempt to leave once he hears the sound of an alarm. If he thinks that you might try to block his exit or that you might have seen him and be able to identify him, you might be in trouble. *Give him the opportunity to leave.* If you feel more secure with your loaded gun then take it with you to your bedroom and sit there behind the locked door until the police arrive.

When the police arrive, if you have a gun, put it away. Do not answer the door with a gun in your hand. If the police see you with a gun in your hand and they are nervous, they might shoot you. Also, you will spend more time proving that it is a legal weapon than the burglar would spend explaining why he was in your home. You do not want to start out calling the police about a burglar and end up being arrested for illegal possession of a weapon. If the police ask if you have a firearm, show them your gun and its permit.

If You Have Been Burglarized

This section might be the least reassuring part of this book. I wish I could tell you that there is a simple solution that will minimize your loss. If you carry out the suggestions I make on page 109, you will minimize your losses.

The procedure that you should follow if you have been burglarized depends on when it occurs and how you discover it. If you are returning home and discover a door opened or a window broken indicating a burglary, *get out.* Don't follow your initial instinct to rush in and see how much damage is done or what is missing. Leave immediately and go to the nearest neighbor. Call the police and let them know where you are. When they arrive, let them go into your home and check it out carefully. The criminal could still be inside. Your return might have caught him in the act or even blocked his escape. You don't want to be the one to find this out.

If you're at home and discover it in the morning when you get up, there is little chance that the burglar is still around. Just to make sure, call the police immediately. Don't touch anything and wait to see what they tell you to do.

Now get out your inventory list and photographs and make a list of everything that is missing. Check everything. Sometimes burglars are very neat and it is weeks before you notice that your pearl necklace is missing from under your night clothes in the drawer. After determining exactly what is missing and what damage is done, give a copy of the list to the police and call your insurance agent. Do not straighten up the house until the police have completed their investigation and say that it's okay to do so. If there is any physical damage including vandalism, take photographs. These are helpful later in determining how much damage the burglar actually did.

Please don't become too upset about the police's attitude or treatment of the crime. Of course, to you this is the worst thing that has ever happened. To the police this might just be another burglary — one of several hundred that year. Most of the time they are sympathetic but you can't help but get hardened after seeing so much crime and knowing that even if you do all your work correctly and catch the culprit, he will probably be out on the streets in a short time.

Don't expect the treatment that is always shown on T.V. Your local police are probably understaffed and don't have all the sophisticated equipment necessary to do an extensive investigation for a crime like burglary. They will do the best that they can with what they have. They might not take fingerprints. Many times this is because they are not trained to take them, don't have the equipment, nor could they do anything with the prints if they had them. The probability of catching a hit-and-miss burglar on fingerprints is very small. If each small police department had to conduct the type of investigation that is shown on T.V. for every little burglar, you would need thousands more police and taxes would be unbearable.

It's up to you to protect yourself by keeping accurate records and descriptions of your valuables. Remember, with the insurance company, you must prove ownership of an item including date and place of purchase and purchase price. Often original sales slips are required or verification from the store where it was purchased. Don't be afraid to ask the store for help. They often keep very accurate sales records for years and are usually willing to help a customer find proof of purchase. I wouldn't count on them only though.

The insurance company will depreciate virtually every item that you lose. Often the depreciated value of an item such as a typewriter or wristwatch is so low that you can't even replace the item lost. The problem is that the purpose of insurance, to quote the law, is "to put you back in the condition you were in before you suffered the loss." This is rarely the case. If a typewriter is depreciated to the point where you cannot replace it with one of equal quality and condition, you are the one who has lost. It's no different than it is with cars. It makes no difference to the insurance company that you took great care of your car so that it was in showroom condition. It was a 1968 Chevy so the book says that it was worth $1500 and that's all that you get. That is why I emphasize the photographs and accurate records of purchase value. If you are going to have to fight for every penny you get, you better have good weapons.

Be sure to check the coverage of your insurance policy. Many have limits on jewelry and cash. Certain collectibles like rare coins, guns, or paintings aren't covered at all. They require a special rider that, of course, costs more. The riders are generally a lot cheaper, however, than the loss of such valuable items.

Having an alarm system is no guarantee that you will not have a loss, but if it has been designed correctly and scares the burglar off it could hold those losses to a minimum.

Unfortunately the recovery rate of stolen items is miserable. The main reason is that many of us have an attitude that if someone offers us a great bargain "don't ask where it came from, just grab it." If a friend or even a stranger says that he can get you a portable color T.V. for $100, we all know that it's too good to be true let alone honest. Yet many of us will buy it and figure, "Why not? Somebody else will get the bargain."

If instead of buying these items, everyone would call the police and tell them about this great bargain, a lot of the people who break into your home and mine would either lose their outlet to sell the stolen items or maybe even get caught. Many of us don't realize that if you make such a purchase you can be named for "receiving stolen goods." This is a criminal offense which could send you to jail.

There was an old story that circulated in my neighborhood when I was a kid and maybe you've already heard it. There were these two men. One had a Corvette and wanted a special high performance transmission to couple to his fuel-injected 327 cubic inch engine. The other had a hot Chevy with a great transmission but a lousy engine. They both contacted a man from "midnight auto supply." The next night the Corvette was stolen and so was the Chevy. When they were found, the Corvette was missing its engine and the Chevy was missing its transmission. You guessed it. Soon came a call from the "midnight auto dealer" to each man stating that their parts were in. What could they do? They knew that they were going to get stolen parts. The irony was that the two men were best friends. Get the idea?

False Alarms

The first thing is to realize that you *will* have a false alarm. It is virtually impossible to eliminate them entirely. The goal should be to limit the number of false alarms to as few as possible.

Let's talk about the different types of false alarms and discuss them separately. First there is a false alarm due to a malfunction in the system itself. Equipment false alarms are most often caused by voltage surges which are normally generated by electrical storms. When I say often, I don't mean that they occur every time there is an electrical storm. You might have one or two of these during the entire life of your system. The number of these false alarms can be reduced when initially selecting your system. The better brand-name systems represent extensive experimentation in the field of electrical disturbances and blocking circuits are incorporated into their central processors to prevent false alarms caused by electrical surges.

The next type of false alarm is the one that *you* accidentally trigger. I'll give you some examples. You get up in the morning and let out the dog or cat but forget to turn off the alarm. Everyone in the neighborhood will know that you forgot. You return home and forget that the person at home may have already set the alarm. When you enter through a protected door the alarm isn't going to know that it's you. Instead it will assume that you are a burglar. After all, he doesn't have a key to turn off the alarm either.

There are more false alarms caused by the owner of the alarm system than I have time to list here. The way to prevent most of these is by learning to live with the system. When you received your first bicycle, during those first shaky rides you fell off several times. Of course, you fell off more in the beginning than you do now. The reason is that you have practiced to the point where you don't have to think about every move. You simply react. An alarm system is similar. After a short time of living with it, you will automatically set it before going to bed and turn it off first thing in the morning without really thinking about it. The more time you own it, the less of an imposition it will be on your life-style.

Let me give you one warning. Do not start to get careless about locking doors just because you have an alarm system. Some people think that they don't really have to lock their doors now because the alarm system will protect them. The nice part of an alarm system is that it will protect you when you have forgotten to lock a door. If a burglar still decides to come in through that unlocked door there is nothing the alarm system can do to prevent him from grabbing something valuable near that entrance and running out with it. Another good reason is that if a friend or relative should visit your home while you are out, he may simply walk in through the unlocked door. He would have a very embarrassing time trying to explain to the police what he was doing in your home.

Now let's assume that you do get a false alarm for whatever reason — what should you do? You should turn off the alarm and go immediately to the front door. Go outside, in plain sight of your neighbors, and wave so that they know that it was only a mistake. If you think you will feel foolish, try explaining to the police when they arrive what happened. Remember, some areas of the country have a fine that you must pay if the police respond to a false alarm at your home.

The procedure just recommended has worked for many of my own friends. The same procedure should be followed if it is in the middle of the night. Turn on the porch lights, go outside, and let your neighbors know that it was an error and you are okay. You may have to explain to some of them the next day, but remember it might only happen once or twice over the years unless you are very careless.

If your system has an automatic dialer, you should immediately call the police and tell them what happened. This will save them the effort of checking it out. Don't forget, although this section on false alarms might be discouraging, it is not a major problem. You will get used to your alarm system quickly, and false alarms will no longer be a problem.

13 | What Can I Do With or Without an Alarm System?

There are many things you can do to improve the security of your home with or without an alarm system. These things will make it more difficult for a burglar to break into your home.

Decals

One thing that can be done is to use warning decals that tell everyone that your home is protected by an alarm system.

There is a great deal of debate over whether to do this. Some people say this is going to tell a burglar you have something worth stealing and the decals are actually an advertisement to this effect. Another argument is if decals alone would work, why bother installing an alarm system?

We will examine these arguments one at a time. The comment that you are inviting a burglar to try your home, in my opinion, is a bunch of horsefeathers. Remember what I said about the professional already knowing what is in the house that he selects to break into? Well, merely posting decals isn't going to make him think differently. The majority of burglaries committed each year are by hit-and-miss amateurs. Knowing this, I can't see this type of amateur trying to take on a burglar alarm system. You must try to put yourself in the position of one of these criminals. If you were going to break into a house and saw decals on the windows and doors stating that the premises are protected by an alarm system, what would you do? If you had even the slightest intelligence, you would walk down the street and select another dark house to try. These amateurs wouldn't even try to defeat the simplest alarm system. They are "quick-hit artists" and deactivating alarm systems is not part of their method of operation. The more a burglar knows about alarm systems, the more professional he is and the less likely he is to select our homes to hit.

I recommend that you purchase some alarm decals. Stick them on every window or door that a burglar is likely to try to break open. Please don't try to hide them because you think that they take away from the beauty of your home. A burglar is not likely to shine a flashlight all over the window to see if the owner has a hidden warning decal in some obscure spot.

Decals should be placed on all windows and doors at ground level. Don't worry about windows that would require an extension ladder to reach. Not many hit-and-miss burglars carry around extension ladders. Placing your decals in a corner of a window or door so they won't be noticed is fine if you don't want the burglar to see them.

Place decals in the spot that the burglar is most likely to look first. This is usually directly in line with the handle or window lock. Place them on the window right behind the latch. This will also make it more difficult for the burglar to see if you accidentally left that latch undone. Always buy extra decals and put them away. Eventually, the ones you have applied will sun fade. It does become rather obvious if you have several different types of decals on your windows.

For those who think this won't work, what if it doesn't? He was going to break into your house anyway. At least with the decals, if they do scare him off, you are ahead of the game. The problem is, as with alarm systems, you really don't know if they scare off a burglar — you only know when they don't.

Door Locks

Although locks are expensive to purchase and have installed, they are probably one of your better investments for the money. They are a definite deterrent, if installed properly. The lock is only as strong as the door and frame on which it is mounted. You can install the best lock money can buy, but if it's on a cheaply constructed door, one or two kicks and the door is open anyway.

If the lock can be unlocked from the inside without a key, it should be installed in a door that has no windows which, if broken, would allow the burglar to reach in and unlock the door.

Don't forget the door can be solid but if there are small glass panels or a small window right next to it, these can be broken to reach the lock.

The lock should be the "dead bolt" type. (See drawing on this page.)

The dead bolt has two advantages. One is that it has a long hardened-steel bolt that goes through the thin framing lumber used on the frame of a door, right into the heavy wood studs. This bolt makes it very difficult to kick the door open.

The second advantage is that the locking mechanism used is the tumbler type. It actually requires key rotation to move the bolt. Pushing on the bolt with a thin metal blade or credit card will not cause the bolt to move in. This is not the case with the standard spring-latch locks used in so many homes. (See drawing on this page.)

The Dead Bolt Lock

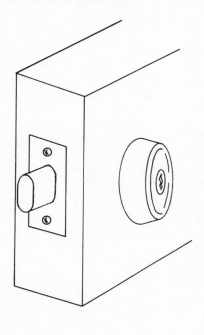

Standard Spring-Latch Door Lock

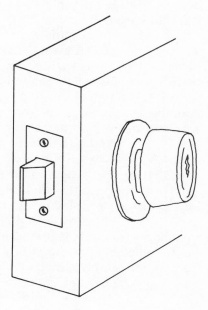

If you are still concerned about the strength of the frame around the door, ask your local locksmith about steel "kick plates." These are steel plates that are screwed into the frame on the side where the bolt goes through into the stud framing. If someone tries to kick the door open, the force of their kick is spread over a much greater area. Kick plates are very effective and I strongly recommend their use in high crime areas.

There are two basic types of deadbolt lock mechanisms. One type has a key slot on the outside of the house and a knob on the inside. The other has key slots on both the inside and outside of the house (double-keyed). Double-keyed locks are commonly used on doors with windows to prevent someone breaking the glass and reaching through to unlock the door.

Warning. If you choose to use a deadbolt that has key slots on both sides you should first check with the town in which you reside to see if there are any ordinances concerning their use. Some localities require that you have at least one door that does not require a key on the inside so that you can't become locked inside your home during a fire. In a panic situation you might not be able to find the keys.

If you decide to use double-keyed locks, you must decide what will be done with the keys. The most secure method is to carry them with you. Even if you have all the locks keyed the same, this can be quite a problem. Women rarely carry their keys on their person, so that if an emergency occurred and the key were needed, it would have to be found first.

One option is to hang the key on a nail next to the door so that it will always be there when you need it. Don't forget, however, that burglars are people, too. They know that this is done. Many times they will break out a window, reach in, and feel around for the key to unlock the door. If you want to hang the key near the door, hang it in a location that will be far from the reach of any windows in the door or windows that are adjacent to it.

You also have to think of your children, when you use double-keyed locks. Not only do they have to carry this key, but the keys that you hang next to the doors must be at a level where they can reach them. In the event of a fire, you wouldn't want them locked inside the home.

Proper installation of locks is important, but proper installation of doors is just as important. Be sure that the door is not installed so that the hinges are on the outside. If this is done, a burglar can simply punch out the hinge pins and take the door off the hinges. The best lock in the world won't prevent this. All hardware on the door should be installed in a way that the burglar can't simply use a screwdriver and disassemble your door from the outside.

Sliding Glass Doors

With the advent of patios and family rooms, sliding glass doors have become more and more popular. These doors provide great views of nature and let in enormous amounts of light but with every advantage comes some disadvantages. Sliding glass doors have become one of the easiest ways into a home.

These doors have some inherent disadvantages. One is that they usually have inferior locking devices. The lock on your door should be examined carefully. Rarely can these locks resist prying. Many can be opened simply by pounding on the outside of the door near the lock. As better doors are designed, their locks are becoming more elaborate. There are also some excellent locks that can be installed on these doors. They will increase your security many times over.

If you wish to do the job as cheaply as possible, there is a rather inexpensive method available. Simply cut a piece of 1" x 2" lumber slightly smaller than the distance between the doorjamb and the sliding door when fully closed. This piece of lumber can then be laid into the track where the door slides, preventing the door from being opened. It's extremely effective.

There are more sophisticated and attractive methods of preventing a sliding glass door from being pried open. Most good hardware stores stock a bar that attaches on the middle of the jamb on the side that is stationary. A small clip is screwed above this bar on the same jamb. When the bar is not in use, it can be held in the upright position by the clip. When security is needed, the door is closed and the bar lowered from its upright position and snapped into a second clip on the frame of the sliding door. With this metal bar across the opening, the door cannot be opened. This also solves the problem of what to do with the piece of 1" x 2" wood when the door is open.

Sliding glass doors have another weakness that the average owner doesn't realize unless he has watched his door being installed. The frame is installed first and then the doors are dropped into place. To take them out again, all that one must do is pry them up from the bottom and pull the bottom outward. The upper track is not only deep enough for the door but it is deep enough to allow the door to be lifted up enough to clear the retainers in the lower track. This makes installation at the job possible.

Fortunately, there is also a rather easy and cheap method of solving this problem. Simply take an electric drill and drill three or four evenly spaced holes into the upper track between the track guides. (See drawing on this page.)

Now take some sheet-metal screws long enough so when they are screwed into the holes they will extend down toward the top of the sliding glass door just enough to clear the upper track. Test your job by gently pulling the door across. If it bumps

Sliding Glass Doors

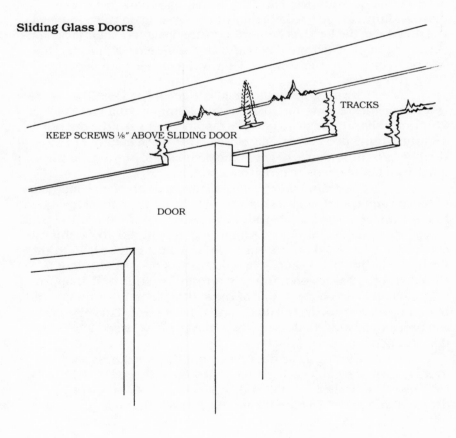

KEEP SCREWS ⅛″ ABOVE SLIDING DOOR

TRACKS

DOOR

into one of the screw heads, give that screw some more turns until it clears the door. These screws will now prevent the door from being pried out of its track.

Window Latches

All windows in your home should be locked — first, for security, and second, most locking systems make the window stay tighter in the frame, preventing cold air from seeping into your home. Some windows, if not locked, will gradually slide down from the top. Ironically, this is where all the heat is located in your rooms — at the ceiling. There are as many styles of windows as there are homes, so I will speak about the most common type. This is generally referred to as a "double-hung" window, where the windows slide up and down, in tracks, over each other. They are usually held in place by a latch. (See drawing on this page.)

This type of latch is easily defeated. Some burglars slide a thin metal blade between the two sashes and simply push the latch around to the open position. Others simply break the window near the latch, reach in, and unlatch it.

Standard Window Latch — Double-Hung Window

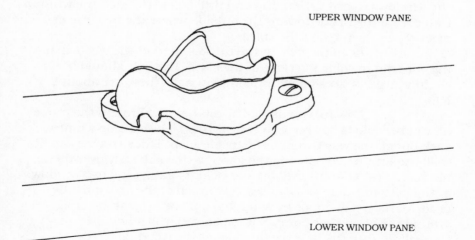

UPPER WINDOW PANE

LOWER WINDOW PANE

Standard Double-Hung Window

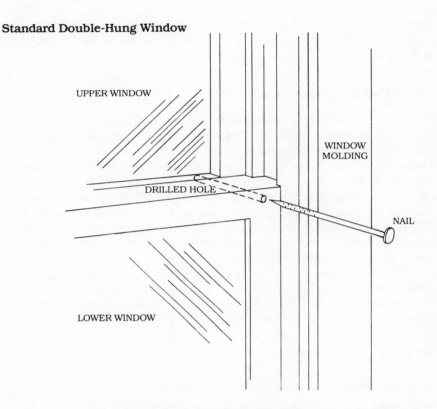

If your windows are double hung and have wooden frames, there is a very inexpensive method of securing them. With the windows closed, take a drill and drill a hole through the window frame from the inside toward the outside where the two frames meet. (See drawing on this page.)

Keep the hole in the thickest part of the wood, making sure not to come too close to the glass. The hole should be slightly larger than an 8 penny common nail. These are about 2½" long.

Be sure you don't drill all the way through the frame. All you need do is go about halfway through the outside window sash but all the way through the inside sash. This distance can be easily determined by raising the lower sash completely over the upper sash. Now take the drill bit and hold it against the two windows at the bottom where you can see how much of the drill must be used. Mark this distance by wrapping a piece of masking tape around the bit at that point. Now when you drill a hole, just push the drill in until the tape barely touches the wood.

After drilling the hole through the inside frame and halfway through the outer frame (the window should still be closed), insert the nail. Now, if someone tries to get into your home, the only way is to break out all the glass. You might say that this is crazy to force him to break out the glass entirely but it makes a lot of noise. No burglar likes to make noise so it is a real deterrent.

Remember to pull out the nail when trying to open the window yourself. Some people forget and think that the window is stuck. They give it a hard hit and break the glass.

Window Locks

Again, there are many different types of window locks. I will discuss just one of the more popular types. I haven't really experienced any real advantage of one type over another. You should ask a locksmith if you have any technical questions.

The lock is only as strong as the window frame on which it is mounted. (See drawing on this page.)

The locking mechanism shown is fairly simple and very secure. When this lock is set, a metal bolt holds the window in place. These locks can also be keyed alike so that you need only one key. Window locks have the same disadvantage as a door with a

Double-hung Window Locking Latch

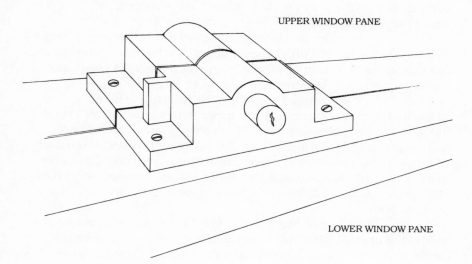

UPPER WINDOW PANE

LOWER WINDOW PANE

double tumbler lock. If you have to get out quickly and can't find the key, you'll have no choice but to break the glass. The advantage is that glass is easy to break compared to pounding your way through a solid wood or metal door.

Lighting

From the standpoint of cost versus protection and in spite of the soaring costs of electricity, lighting is still the best deterrent to burglary. It is extremely effective because it can reveal the criminal's presence and make it possible for him to be identified, caught, or even killed. On any given night, a burglar will select a less expensive, poorly lighted house over a more expensive well-lighted one.

The major problem is to use light effectively and efficiently. This is a task that may appear, on the surface, to be rather simple to accomplish but actually is very complicated. There are experts in the area of lighting who know the type of fixtures available, proper lighting levels for various situations, and proper wattage for maximum efficiency. Lighting design is not something that I recommend for everyone to try. Contact a lighting specialist. In the long run you will recover any additional costs by savings through efficient lighting design. If cost is a major problem, contact your local utility and ask for help from one of their lighting engineers. If at first they refuse, send them a few letters and direct them to the top management. Often they would rather have someone help you than hear your complaints.

In order for lighting to be helpful in reducing burglaries it must be turned on at night. Timers and light controllers are invaluable tools. You might forget to turn on the lights out back but a photosensitive light controller will never forget.

If you choose to design the lighting yourself, use as many mercury vapor and sodium vapor lights as possible. These lights don't cast dark shadows. Shadows are also places where someone can hide. Sodium vapor lights are being used extensively in large cities. These are the weird orange-colored lights. This frequency of light seems to cast the least shadow. For the amount of light provided these lights are also cheaper to operate than incandescent ones.

Indoor lighting is also important. Always provide a method of operating lights covering areas that may be potential break-in points from a location that does not put you in danger. It's ridiculous to have to walk through a dark basement to get to a light switch. Outside area flood lights should be controlled from an area that does not require you to light up half the house to reach the switch to turn on these lights.

As suggested in another chapter, I think that it would be very valuable to be able to control the outside lights from the master bedroom. These switches aren't that difficult to install. If you don't think you can do it, save your money and have these security improvements done one at a time. Eventually your home will have most of them installed and it will be much safer from burglary.

Fences

Fences provide both privacy and protection but careful consideration must be given to the selection of the type of fence for your home so as not to offend your neighbor or make your home look like "Fort Apache." If your primary reason for installing a fence is for the protection of your home, **I do not recommend** installing one. First, they are too expensive for the amount of protection they provide. Second, the type that gives the greatest protection against burglary you wouldn't want around your home.

If you are going to erect a fence to meet zoning laws which require you to provide protection against accidental incursion into your pool, there are other considerations to make. One is to make sure you have checked the local zoning ordinance and are sure about the height and setback requirements. Next, check with your neighbors and show them a picture, if possible, of the type of fence you intend to erect. If they have some objection to the appearance of such a fence, ask them to make a suggestion of a design that they think would better complement the neighborhood. If this fence is more expensive, it is perfectly reasonable to ask if they would be willing to share a portion of the additional cost of such a fence.

You must be extremely careful about getting into a "fence war." I don't think that it's worth it to have your fence but lose your neighbors. This is all too often the case when someone acts without thinking. Once your fence is installed it's too late to change it — the war has started.

You should also remember that a fence can block your neighbors' vision of people entering your home. This may seem convenient until the person they can't see is a burglar. Most often the best protection you can have is a neighbor curious enough to watch your home. They are often the first ones to report someone going in when you are not at home.

Check with the township to see if there is a regulation stating which side of the fence must be on the outside — the finished or unfinished side. People have had fences installed with the finished side on the inside because they don't want the ugly side in their view. After the entire thing is up, the township zoning officer comes around and tells them that there is an ordinance requiring the finished side to be on the outside. This mistake can be very expensive.

If you must put up a fence for your pool and for privacy, you have the option to fence only that area immediately around the pool. By doing this you might not block your neighbor's view of your home. This method also reduces the cost of the fence.

If you do decide to fence your entire property, try to have the gates in a section of the fence that is not only convenient for you, but in a section where your neighbor can see someone going into your yard. This will give you an additional margin of protection. If you erect a fence that is so high and solid that no neighbor can see inside, you have a problem. Once a burglar gets inside, he can chop down your door with an ax and nobody will know that it's not you working.

Dogs

I have had a great deal of experience with dogs. The question arises — Should I get a dog to protect my property? The answer is no — definitely not. This is the wrong reason to acquire a dog. The only way that the dog and its owners are going to be happy is if the dog was acquired for the right reasons.

For the average owner, purchasing a dog with the idea that you will be able to have it attack-trained and at the same time a good pet is just plain crazy. Along with this pet comes responsibility. The dog requires care, affection, and exercise. In return, it will usually be a loving and loyal member of your family.

Without writing another book on dogs, since there are already many great ones, let me give you a few warnings:

Taking a trip will no longer be simple. A dog must eat every day and get some exercise. Although this might be supplied by a qualified kennel, your dog might decide that no one else but you can do it. Dogs aren't like children; if they get something like this in their heads they will even starve to death before taking food from a stranger.

To constantly keep a dog on a chain is cruel treatment. This can make some dogs very vicious. Dogs are normally sociable. If every time they see someone they run toward him, reach the end of their chain, and get jerked off their feet, they will make a decision. You might say they will learn. Yes, they will, but it might be the wrong thing. They might associate the appearance of a human with pain so they will begin to hate the sight of people. This has been the cause of some very vicious dogs and the owner never knows why.

Keeping a dog inside a fence can have a similar effect. All day it is surprised by these sudden noises that can't be seen. It finally begins to fear them and can become a constant barker or worse, a biter.

Having a dog attack-trained or attempting to do it yourself is a risky endeavor. An attack-trained dog is considered a weapon, just like a gun, in the eyes of the law. The major difference is with a gun, someone must intentionally aim it at someone to do them harm. Attack-trained dogs are an "always loaded" gun.

My recommendation is don't purchase a dog with protection in mind. Instead, purchase a dog with the intention of making it a member of your family. Better yet get one from the S.P.C.A. and save its life. If it becomes protective of your property and family, consider that a bonus.

Guns

This is a subject that often gets caught up in arguments involving a great deal of emotion. Let me state right up front that I do support the right to private ownership of guns and I do not ever want to see this right revoked. Supporting this as a constitutional right does not mean that I believe that every citizen should sleep with a loaded gun under his pillow. There are some people I would not want to see with a gun in their hands. There are many more people who I don't like to see get behind the wheel of a car either.

My major objection to guns in the hands of the average person is that a good gun costs about as much as a good alarm system. The owner of an alarm system doesn't have to take it out periodically and practice with it. If he makes a mistake nobody gets hurt.

If you choose a gun for your home protection, you must decide where you will keep it so that you can get to it on short notice. If you keep it loaded (which is insane), how do you prevent someone from getting hurt with it? If you don't keep it loaded, where do you keep the shells? How quickly can you find them and load your weapon in the dark? Most burglars aren't polite enough to give you time to find the ammunition and load the weapon so that you can shoot them.

Let's just assume that you have a solution for all these problems. It's 3 a.m. and you hear a noise downstairs. You get out of bed quietly and search through the closet shelf where you are positive you put the gun last month after cleaning it. You load it successfully in the dark.

Now what do you do? Do you go out into the hall and flick on the lights? Do you go downstairs in the dark so that he can't see you? Where is he, behind that chair or door, around the next corner, in the family room? Should you turn on lights as you go through the house? He knows where you are! If you do see him will you have the nerve to shoot? Will he shoot you? What does the law in your state say about shooting him?

Instead of having this never-ending argument, I'll tell you what I think you should do. As I mentioned before, on hearing a noise that you believe may be a burglar, call the police. Next, get your family into your bedroom and lock the door. Turn on your lights, open up the window, and scream to your neighbors for help. A burglar with any sense is running away by this time. When you scream, scream a neighbor's name so he will know that it's not just a bunch of people fooling around outside.

When the police arrive, throw them your keys and let them do the job for which you pay them. They are the professionals. They will check the entire premises and let you know what has happened with no risk to you.

The above procedure serves two purposes. First, it prevents you from shooting a relative who might have come in late and it prevents you from getting killed. I don't believe that it makes good sense to try to play "shoot-out at the OK Corral" with a burglar. He has two almost insurmountable advantages: he *knows* where you are and you *don't know* where he is.

Landscaping

For too many years, the only consideration given to landscaping was how to make your home more attractive. Now, the primary importance should be shifted from just beauty to beauty that does not provide a nest of hiding places for burglars. There are many ways of accomplishing this goal. What is a small bush or tree today will be a large bush or tree in a few years. If it is placed in a location where it can be used to conceal the burglar while he attempts to break into your house then it's improperly placed. If that tree becomes a ladderway to your windows, it is also placed improperly.

For the average person, landscaping is something that is difficult if not impossible. Now to complicate it with these requirements makes it more of a problem. Most of us will consult a landscaper for help. If you don't want to spend that money, simply ask the nursery where you buy your bushes what types will stay low and still look attractive. There are also methods of pruning most plants to control their size. The nurseries know most of these methods.

If you get a bid on landscaping from a contractor, ask him for a plan that will show the actual location of the items he plans to plant. If you have questions about maintenance of a particular type of plant, this is the time to ask, not after it is planted. If a plant seems to be located in an area that you believe provides a hiding place for a burglar, ask the architect for a suggestion of how to remove this problem. Just don't let anyone convince you that your home can't look attractive unless you have large bushes and trees growing right up against it. A tree planted several feet from the house might look unusual for several years, but it will grow and then you can trim those branches that would allow someone access to one of your windows.

Telephones

Many families in the U.S. today have more than one telephone. If you have several extensions of a single line, **I recommend** that these be a jack-type installation. The new modular-type telephones have a small plug that is very helpful.

The reason I am concerned about extension telephones is that if a burglar has some experience, he will, immediately on entering the home, remove the telephone from the hook. By doing this he will prevent you from making a telephone call to the police.

One solution to this problem is to open the window and scream your head off. Another is to simply unplug the most obvious telephone downstairs before retiring for the evening. If you are one of those parents that has yielded to the request for a separate line for your child, you should have this phone installed in your bedroom, not in the child's bedroom. By doing this you have a second line that can't be interrupted by the burglar and also you can maintain some degree of control over its use. Your child still gets the privacy that he or she desires, but the amount of use can be controlled and those late night calls can be eliminated.

Radios

With the advent of the transistor, the power requirement of radios has been decreased to the point where it can't be detected in the average electric bill. Because of this, they are excellent as a method of giving a house that "lived-in" sound.

When you are out for the evening or even for a short period, it's advisable to leave a radio on in some room of the house. If a forced entry does occur while you are gone, it's possible that the burglar, hearing the radio, will believe that someone is at home or at least not want to take the chance and he'll leave. Don't use a T.V. for this purpose. They are much too expensive to operate. Even the transistor models can use 800 watts of power.

Timers

Although timers are not effective against a more experienced burglar, they work well on the hit-and-miss version. Two timers placed in areas of the home that you would normally expect to use during the night can give the home a lived-in appearance. A good place to use a timer is in the family room and either an upstairs bedroom or a bathroom. Using two timers would be better than using one because it makes the place look as though there is really someone home.

The timer settings should be logical to reflect the normal use of the home. For instance, during the winter months, the family room light might go on at 6 p.m. in the Northeast (adjust for other time zones). This light might conceivably stay on until 11 p.m.

At the same time a timer in the bedroom could turn on a light at 11 p.m. and turn it off at 11:30 or so. You can make up your own time patterns but they should stay logical. With the newer designs in timers there is a setting for random selection of on-and-off times. You might not want to use this selection in the family room but why not in the bathroom?

Photosensitive Light Controllers

I prefer the use of photosensitive light controllers for outdoor lighting. The reason is that outdoor lights are so easy to forget to turn on. They aren't very logical to use inside except in an entryway where you might want a light to be turned on at dark and not go out until daytime again.

Photosensitive light controllers have some disadvantages also. One major one is the light they control can activate them to turn off. This often happens when the controller is poorly placed and perceives too much light from the bulbs it controls. An action called "pumping" can occur. This is a common error when people use them on outside lights. Many of the better controllers have a built-in time delay to allow the controller to last through temporary darkness caused by a cloud passing over the sun. The problem is that when you are setting these up, you do it during the day. At night when it gets dark, the controller turns on the lights. The light from the spotlights causes the controller to think that it's daytime again and the controller turns off the lights once again. This will cause the lights to blink on and off all night. Never assume that you set them up correctly. Go outside and watch them for a period of ten or fifteen minutes. This period is long enough to outlast any time delay that might be built-in.

Photosensitive light controllers have the advantage of being independent of losses in voltage. If the power is lost in a timer for some period, the entire timing sequence is lost. Once the power returns to the photosensitive light controller it simply goes back to its job of looking for the presence of light.

Hiding Places

Everyone has his or her favorite hiding place in the home. We are all certain that no one could ever find it. You would be surprised just how obvious some of these hiding places are. Some of them have actually become traditions that have been practiced for generations. I suggest that if you are using one of the traditional hiding places you should give serious thought to changing it. You can bet your last dollar that if I know them and can publish them in this book, they are not very big surprises to the average burglar.

I'll tell you some of the most common ones and hope that if I reveal one that you are presently using, this will be all the proof you need to think if something new.

Keys: under the mat; on the step or landing; in a flower pot; on the windowsill; in a planter; above the door on the frame; in a glass in the china closet; on a hook in the kitchen; under a rock next to the door; in a magnetic can attached to the bottom of the mailbox; hanging on a chain in a bush next to the door.

Guns: in a drawer of the nightstand; under the clothes in your dresser; on the top shelf of your closet under some clothes; between the mattress and the box spring; in a shoe or boot under the bed; behind a book on the bookshelf near the bed.

Jewelry: in a jewel box on top of the dresser; sitting out on top of the dresser; in a velvet box under your negligee; in a plastic bag in the freezer (if you are going to do this, at least put it in an empty vegetable box and pack it with paper so it doesn't rattle); in a plastic bag hanging on the toilet bowl reservoir.

Money: in the top dresser drawer; in a jewelry box; in the china closet; in a tea kettle near the kitchen sink; in glass bottles, jars, and banks; in an envelope in the linen drawer in the dining room; between the mattress and the box spring; in a shoebox in the closet.

Most hiding places depend on the size and type of article to be hidden. Jewelry can be easily hidden because of its size but remember you don't want to select a location that could be easily stumbled on by your kids while playing (e.g., in an old cigar box in the bottom of a closet). Kids play in the strangest places. You also want to avoid hiding it in something that could accidentally be thrown out during spring cleaning. All too often someone has hidden something in some old article and had it thrown out by another member of the family, just to find out a year later.

A man I once knew had a collection of silver coins in an old cloth bag in the bottom of his closet. One day when he wasn't home, a delivery man stopped and had something that had been sent C.O.D. His son didn't want to send back the item so he remembered the bag of coins that he had once seen in the bottom of Dad's closet. You guessed it. He paid the delivery man with these old silver coins. We don't know to this day whether the delivery man knew their real value.

You might be wondering where it is safe to hide something. The answer is anywhere that is safe. What I mean is only you can decide what seems safe for the item in question. If it is an item such as a collection you are just saving and don't need to get at regularly, the attic is an excellent place. Label it with something like Reader's Digest Books or whatever you'll remember. Very few burglars ever try to search attics because they are so cluttered with junk. Just keep in mind that attic temperatures can get up over 140° F even in the winter.

Safes

Safes come in all sizes and shapes depending on what you want them to protect. Most freestanding safes for the home are not intended to protect your valuables against theft. Instead they are intended to protect important papers against burning during a fire.

I was recently in a local department store when they were having a sale that included safes. I saw a man having one brought to his car in a shopping cart. It took two men to load it into his car. I hope that the man wasn't buying it to prevent theft. If he can carry it out of the store, a thief can carry it out of his home. This is generally what is done to residential safes. They are toted away where the burglar has all day to pound on them with a sledge-hammer.

Wall and floor safes are expensive and difficult to install. Often they are beaten open with tools supplied right in the home of the owner (a cold chisel and a sledgehammer).

The best and safest thing to do is to rent a safe deposit box in a local bank. The cost is tax deductible. If you do have a safe deposit box, be sure to check with your attorney to see if you should have a "power of attorney" for each person who uses the box. Many times a person dies and his or her estate is not settled. During this time, which can be months or years, there may be items in the safe deposit box that are yours and that you might need, but because the box is sealed on the death of the owner, it is impossible for you to get into it.

If you are determined to use your own safe and you have an alarm system, it isn't difficult to extend the protection of that system to the safe. This can be as simple as placing a mat in front of the safe or using a contact provided in the safe door for this purpose. Also be sure that the safe has a high thermal rating. It does no good to have your safe survive a fire to open it and find that all the items inside were fried to a crisp.

Now you can see that there are many things you can do with or without an alarm system. Get started doing them and you may prevent your home from being burglarized.

Uses for the Sick or Elderly

If you are now young and in good health, the next point of discussion may be wasted, but you should remember you won't always remain this way. There may come a day when you need to be able to call for assistance for a serious problem, such as a heart attack or a fall.

Most of the alarm systems that I have been describing can be equipped with a small hand-held transmitter that activates the alarm. These systems can also be used to activate dialers. Because people are living longer, there are many more older people at home alone for extended periods of time. Your alarm system can be adapted to provide an extra benefit that might save the life of someone you love.

Let's just suppose that one of your parents is living alone at home and has a heart attack or suffers a fall where his mobility is impaired to the point that he cannot reach a telephone to call for help. By simply pressing the button on the small hand-held transmitter he can trigger the burglar alarm system. Someone hearing this would call the police and, upon investigating the cause of the alarm, they would more than likely discover your dad.

If you wanted to ensure that they would know the cause of the alarm, there are two ways to accomplish this. One is to put signs in the window stating "In Case of an Alarm Check Senior Citizen in Residence." This would certainly cause the police to check the house carefully. Another more positive method of accomplishing this job would be to install the transmitter on the second, (interior) zone of the alarm system and have a telephone dialer that would be programmed to call the police and give them a message that medical assistance is needed at the following address.

This method would negate the use of the second zone of security for protection of the premises, but the main reason I **recommend** the second zone is in case no one is going to be home for extended periods. If your parent is staying in the home, you wouldn't be able to use "active" type detection methods nor would you need them. Your parent would report a burglary in progress while he is protected by the first zone of protection.

This is not a feature that you often see employed but it could save a life — the life of someone very important to you.

14 | What Should I Do When Taking a Trip?

When you plan to take a trip which will mean being away from your home for some extended time, there are some things that you should do. You should make some initial checks of the alarm system to make sure that it is functioning properly. These are simple checks. First, you should set the alarm and open a door or window to see that the system sounds an alarm. Next, you should check the battery throw-over system. To do this you must remove the A.C. supply from the system.

There are two ways to do this. The simplest method is usually to pull out the small trickle-charged transformer that feeds the system. If this is a problem, you can open up the control box and remove one of the leads that come from the transformer. They are usually marked "A.C." or "Trans." After you have removed the normal A.C. feed, set the alarm again and open a door or window. This test is to see if the batteries can carry the load of the alarm. Often a battery can maintain enough "surface charge" to light the indicator lights and to arm the system but not enough to power the siren or bell. If the siren or bell sounds very low or doesn't ring at all, the storage battery must be replaced. Be sure to plug the transformer back into the outlet before you do anything else.

There are also precautions that should be taken with or without an alarm system. They are:

1. Try not to tell everyone in the neighborhood that you are going away. If there is a burglar in the neighborhood this is very valuable information. Information like this is often repeated by your friends and sometimes the wrong person hears it.

2. Be sure to have a friend, relative, or neighbor pick up your newspapers and mail. I prefer this method to having these stopped. When you stop normal deliveries you must tell someone for what period and too often this information can get into the wrong hands.

3. Be sure to have someone mow your lawn while you're away. There is no better sign that no one is home than grass two feet tall. If a neighbor isn't willing to help, there are professional lawn care services and you don't have to explain why, just tell them the period that you wish to have this done. Simply consider this part of the trip expense.

4. Most people have a good relationship with their neighbors. If you are one of these lucky people, tell them that you are going away, what kind of activity they can expect to see around your home, and give them the necessary information to get in touch with you in case of an emergency. Tell the neighbors on each side and let them know that they both know. That way they will watch both sides of your home. This is very helpful. There is often no better protection than a watchful neighbor.

Some people like to notify the police. In very small communities where the police know everyone, this is a good idea. They will make a few extra passes by your home while on duty. In a larger community where the police are already overburdened and understaffed, it probably won't be much help. I know this statement won't make me any friends in police stations across the country, but I'm trying to be realistic.

The Town Watch Program

Today people are constantly complaining about their taxes and often one of the first places to take a revenue cut is the police department. They are like the fire company — people only appreciate them when they need them. The police in our community have a large patrol area and not enough officers to perform their jobs to the degree that I'm sure they would like. In spite of this our Town Watch Program has received great cooperation and never have I heard of a complaint about police response. So if you want to help, start a Town Watch Program.

The National Town Watch Association was started in early 1981 by Matt Peskin from Havertown, Pennsylvania. Matt was involved in trying to reduce crime rates in his own area. As an aid in his efforts he published a crime-watch newsletter. He started to run out of material for his newsletter so began to investigate the crime prevention efforts of surrounding communities. He found there were many different organizations, each with similar goals. The real problem was that each was trying to "invent its own wheel." He got together with those involved in the other organizations and formed an association.

The National Town Watch Association is a non-profit organization, made up of a combination of law enforcement representatives, citizens' groups, district coordinators, and volunteer groups involved in crime prevention. The most important characteristic of the association is that those citizens' groups accepted for membership must be affiliated with their local police department.

The program in our township has had enormous success simply because it is run by a few people who are dedicated to the task. In our program there are no patrols. We simply share information and report all unusual people and events to the police. The police are very happy with the program and have given it their fullest cooperation.

The organization has grown and there are some "8–10 million people involved in about 20,000 organized programs across the country" according to Matt Peskin.

The group has received national recognition for its accomplishments. In a letter from the U.S. Department of Justice in 1985, Lois Haight Herrington, Assistant Attorney General, said, "We are confident that recent declines in the crime rate across the country are in large part the result of citizens watching out for one another, keeping an eye on their neighborhoods and sending the message to the criminal element that the law-abiding public is watching. Even more importantly, we believe that such declines will continue as more and more citizens become involved."

In 1986, in a proclamation declaring "National Crime Watch Day" President Reagan said, "We recognize the growth and the proven effectiveness of local crime watch organizations throughout the country. They have played a major role in turning the tide against crime. People working together with their local law enforcement agencies have always been the best deterrent to crime."

These praises aren't just the political speeches that we so often hear aimed at flattering the well-meaning intentions of some public-minded citizen. The accomplishments of town watch organizations have been demonstrated in every area of the country where these programs have been tried. In a report by Dr. John C. Pollock, "The Figgie Report, Reducing Crime in America: Successful Community Effort," *The Police Chief*, December 1983, it was concluded that, "The resurgence of neighborly concern has not only reduced significantly the incidence of crime, as recent FBI statistics confirm, but it has also greatly assuaged the fear of crime so prevalent in our earlier studies. Ironically, we've found that fear can be a good thing if it spurs community response."

I agree that fear is a great incentive. If you don't believe it, ask anyone who has been in combat. They will tell you that fear alone made them perform feats of endurance that they previously thought impossible. But there is another face to fear and that is confidence. I have found that once a crime watch program accomplishes its goal of reducing crime in a neighborhood, the people become confident and feel that they no longer have to participate in the program. After all, "we don't have a crime problem any longer." Well, this can be the fatal error. Once this attitude becomes prevalent, those involved in crime are quick to take advantage. My own neighborhood is experiencing this problem.

Crime prevention is like dieting. Most diets have, as their goal, the removal of excess weight. Once this weight has been removed, most dieters believe that they can return to their previous eating habits. We all know what happens next. Dr. James Corea, a well-known radio personality and nutrition expert in the Philadelphia area, states that he hates the word diet — that we are on a diet every day of our lives. Remembering this is the only way to control weight. He urges people to eat properly. If this were done, "diets" would be unnecessary. He is also quick to recognize that everyone wants the weight control pill that they can simply take and then eat anything they want.

People also want a one-time, simple solution for crime prevention. They want the "cure-all" that they simply apply once and crime is eliminated. As Matt Peskin can tell you — it doesn't exist. A good crime prevention program becomes part of the community and part of our everyday lives. If this is done, crime will seek another area, looking for those who believe in the "one time cure-all."

I encourage you to start a town watch program in your area now, not tomorrow. If one exists — become involved before you are involved. For information about National Town Watch contact: National Association of Town Watch, P.O. Box 769, Havertown, PA 19083.

The Federal Government has also become involved through the U.S. Department of Justice by sponsoring the National Crime Prevention Campaign. The National Crime Prevention Council sponsors programs across the nation and has a number of good

Emergency Information Form

Police

I can be reached at:

_____

_____

Telephone: _____

_____

Address:

_____

_____

_____

From: (Date)   To: (Date)

_____   _____

In Case of Emergency Please Contact:

_____

_____

Telephone: _____

_____

Address:

_____

_____

_____

publications. For additional information on how they can help you and your community write: National Crime Prevention Council, 733 15th Street NW, Suite 540, Washington, DC 20005, Attention: Resource Center, or call: 202-393-7141.

When you go on a trip or plan to be away from your home for an extended period, it is very wise to leave behind essential information so that you can be reached in an emergency, if necessary. The following is a clearly printed form that **I recommend** you use. It should be copied, filled out, and placed on the refrigerator door in plain sight.

This information would be very useful to the police if there was an actual forced entry. The police would enter your home to investigate the premises, and would very likely see the note on the refrigerator.

One problem everyone faces when preparing to leave for vacation is remembering what tasks must be performed before locking the front door. In the interest of saving time I have included a vacation checklist. I recommend making copies of it for future use. Check off each item before leaving.

Vacation Checklist

Did I:

☐ Let someone know where to reach me
☐ Give them dates and itinerary
☐ Turn off the hot water heater
☐ Turn off outside faucets
☐ Turn off the hot and cold water to clothes washer
☐ Lock all windows and doors
☐ Put locking bar in sliding glass doors
☐ Ask someone to get mail and papers
☐ Get someone to mow lawn
☐ Unplug T.V., stereo, video games
☐ Leave on a radio in bedroom
☐ Set light timers
☐ Check alarm system operation
☐ Check alarm battery throw-over system
☐ Get someone to feed dog, cat, bird, hamster, fish
☐ Post information on refrigerator

15 | What Will the Insurance Company Ask?

There is a unique arrangement between you and your insurance company. The stated purpose of insurance is to put you back in the condition that you were in before you sustained the loss. This, unfortunately, is not always the case. The major reason for this problem is depreciation. Many items lost in a fire or stolen in a burglary are not new. Instead they have been in your possession for some time. During this time, it is reasonable to assume that these articles have received some wear or loss of value due to their age. Even though the object still serves you well, it may be virtually worthless on today's market.

For example, let's discuss a manual typewriter. Although this machine serves your needs and was in "like-new" condition. It is doubtful, in the age of electronics, that this manual machine would have much value. It is this argument that often drives a wedge between the insured and the insurer. You must make an effort to understand the position of the insurer. It is the responsibility for the company to pay your claim but not to put you in a better position than you were in before you sustained your loss.

If a fear of depreciation bothers you, there are many insurance companies that have policies that will replace any object with a present-day value. With this type of policy your loss should be virtually eliminated. Of course like any other desirable item it will cost more than a policy without this provision.

Falsifying a Claim

It is often argued that because the insurance company is going to pay you a depreciated value, it is in your best interest to lie about your loss. This is too often done by attempts to exaggerate the value of an item or by claiming the loss of items that weren't even stolen. I cannot state strongly enough — **deception on an insurance claim is a crime.** Don't even think of filing a false or exaggerated claim.

Many insurance policies have a clause to protect the insurance company against just such an event. The clause generally goes something like this:

> This entire policy shall be void if, whether before or after a loss, the insured has willfully concealed or misrepresented any material or circumstance concerning this insurance or the subject thereof, or the interest of the insured therein, or in the case of any fraud or false swearing by the uninsured relating thereto.

I will take the risk of oversimplifying what this clause means — if you lie to the insurance company they don't have to pay you a cent. This seems like an awfully large risk to take.

After Filing a Claim

According to the *Investigators and Adjusters Handbook,* the insurance company will do the following after a claim is filed:

1. Read carefully the statement made by the person filing the claim to determine the value that the insured has placed on the items lost.
2. Make an attempt to confirm the ownership of every item lost as described in the statement filed.
3. Attempt to confirm that the claimed articles actually existed and were in the insured's possession.
4. Verify the value by ascertaining the place of purchase of each article and the purchase price.
5. Use recognized authorities to determine the present-day value of the article lost.
6. Attempt to determine the cost of replacement of such an article on today's market.
7. Obtain a sample of the item lost in the case of goods or stock. This sample will be used to determine the value of the items lost.
8. Interact with the investigating authorities to try to determine the probability of recovering the lost items. In the case of ex-

tremely valuable items they might actually take part in the investigation.

9. Deduct any depreciation for articles where it is appropriate.

In Case of a Burglary

Again, according to the *Investigators and Adjusters Handbook*, the insurance company will want to know the following things:

1. The exact date and time of the burglary or theft
2. The exact location from which the property was stolen
3. A full description of the physical marks of entry or exit, if any
4. The character of the premises, whether a private dwelling, apartment house, condo. etc.
5. Whether the premises were occupied and being lived in by the insured or some member of the household
6. If unoccupied, the length the premises had been vacant
7. A detailed list of the property claimed to have been stolen
8. A complete description of how the crime was committed, if known
9. The exact date, time, and means of notification of the police
10. Copies of the insured's entries in any books, vouchers, receipts, or papers indicating the character and value of the articles missing
11. Dates of purchase and owners of purchased articles
12. Similar insurance policy with any other company
13. Prior burglary loss
14. Members of the insured's household home at the time of the crime
15. Other possible causes contributing to the loss, such as fire, storm, or any similar problem
16. A copy of the police report

The investigator for the insurance company will cooperate with the police to try to recover the stolen items. They will make every attempt to determine the truth in the filing of the report. port.

Warning. Since the police are sure to get involved in a burglary and the fire department in a fire, it is **my recommendation** to be honest. If you feel that an item has been stolen but are not sure, simply list it as possibly stolen. In that way, if the item turns up later, there is no problem with your claim. You must remember that the burden of proof is on you to show that certain items were in your possession and that they originally cost a certain amount. It is not to your advantage to fight the system but instead to use it as it is designed. It is for this reason that **I strongly urge** you to take the time now to complete the forms that are provided in this book. If you follow this procedure you will find that both you and the adjuster will have a better relationship and your loss will be minimized.

Lists

The following list should be completely filled out and dated. I know that it seems like a real chore, but if your home is burglarized or you have a fire, you will find that this is the most valuable time you have ever spent. These lists should be updated whenever you make a purchase of an item that you consider expensive (e.g., furniture, jewelry, furs, guns). The completed copies should be kept in a safe deposit box with your other valuable papers. Another good practice is to take photographs of every room, each wall, every closet. Have these photographs developed (preferably slides because they take up little room and don't get stuck to each other over time). These pictures will go a long way in convincing an insurance company that you really did own the items you are claiming. If you have done some outstanding remodeling to a family room, den, or kitchen, take photographs. These will show the quality of the workmanship better than you can describe. Remember the burden of proof is on you.

Many people think that they can simply remember what valuables they own. If you are one of these people try this test. Pick a reasonably cluttered closet and try to list the things that are in there. You might be missing some very important things. Now multiply this mistake by every closet in the home, the attic, the basement, and the garage, and you'll have some idea of how much money you can lose. The items may be old but you wouldn't throw them away and would want to be paid for them if they were lost in a fire or stolen in a theft.

Take some time and fill out the following lists. The best time to do this is during spring cleaning. You will spend a great deal of time in each room and be able to list the items while in there. Remember, if you don't take the time to do this chore (and you only have to do it once) you may regret it later.

Theft Prone Items

ITEM/BRAND	YEAR PURCH'D	SERIAL NUMBER	EST. VALUE ($)
Collector's Items			
Antiques			
Art Objects			
Figurines			
Paintings			
Other			
Electronic Equipment			
Clocks			

ITEM/BRAND	YEAR PURCH'D	SERIAL NUMBER	EST. VALUE ($)
Electronic Equip. (cont.)			
Clock Radios			
Calculators			
Stereo Equipment			
Tape Recorders			
Televisions			
Computer Equipment			

ITEM/BRAND	YEAR PURCH'D	SERIAL NUMBER	EST. VALUE ($)
Computer Equipment (cont.)			
Electrical Appliances			

ITEM/BRAND	YEAR PURCH'D	SERIAL NUMBER	EST. VALUE ($)
Hobbies/ Collections			
Craft Materials			
Photography			
Musical Instruments			
Toys			

ITEM/BRAND	YEAR PURCH'D	SERIAL NUMBER	EST. VALUE ($)
Other			
Jewelry/Furs			
Bracelets			
Broaches			
Earrings			
Necklaces			

ITEM/BRAND	YEAR PURCH'D	SERIAL NUMBER	EST. VALUE ($)
Jewelry/ Furs (cont.)			
Rings			
Watches			
Other			
Lawn Mowers			

ITEM/BRAND	YEAR PURCH'D	SERIAL NUMBER	EST. VALUE ($)
Power Tools			
Precious Metals			
Sports Equipment			
Bikes			
Bowling			
Fishing			

ITEM/BRAND	YEAR PURCH'D	SERIAL NUMBER	EST. VALUE ($)
Sports Equip. (cont.)			
Golf			
Skiing			
Firearms			
Swim & Diving Gear			
Tennis Equipment			
Motorcycles			
Recreational Vehicles			

Home Inventory

Living Room and Dining Room

NUMBER OF ITEMS	DESCRIPTION OF ITEM	EST. VALUE ($)
	Air-conditioner Window Units	
	Books	
	Bookcases	
	Bric-a-brac	
	Buffet	
	Cabinets and Contents	
	Chairs	
	China	
	Closet Contents	
	Couches	
	Crystal	
	Curtains	
	Desk	
	Fireplace Equipment	
	Lamps	
	Organ	
	Piano	
	Rug	
	Tables	
	Table Linens	
	Wall Shelves	
	Wall Hangings	
	Other:	

ADDITIONAL DESCRIPTION OF ITEMS IF NECESSARY

Family Room

NUMBER OF ITEMS	DESCRIPTION OF ITEM	EST. VALUE ($)
	Air-conditioner Window Units	
	Books	
	Bookcases	
	Bric-a-brac	
	Cabinets and Contents	
	Card Table	
	Chairs	
	Closet and Contents	
	Couches	
	Curtains/Shades	
	Desk	
	Fireplace Equipment	
	Lamps	
	Organ	
	Piano	
	Rugs	
	Tables	
	Wall Shelves	
	Wall Hangings	
	Plants	
	Other:	

ADDITIONAL DESCRIPTION OF ITEMS IF NECESSARY

Bedrooms

NUMBER OF ITEMS	DESCRIPTION OF ITEM	EST. VALUE ($)
	Air-conditioner Window Units	
	Bedding	
	Beds	
	Books	
	Bookcases	
	Bric-a-brac	
	Bureaus and Contents	
	Chairs	
	Chests and Contents	
	Closets and Contents	
	Curtains/Shades	
	Desk	
	Dresser and Contents	
	Dresser Table	
	Lamps	
	Mattresses	
	Rugs	
	Sewing Machine	
	Box Springs	
	Tables	
	Shelving	
	Mirrors	
	Wall Hangings	
	Other:	

ADDITIONAL DESCRIPTION OF ITEMS IF NECESSARY

Bedrooms

NUMBER OF ITEMS	DESCRIPTION OF ITEM	EST. VALUE ($)
	Air-conditioner Window Units	
	Bedding	
	Beds	
	Books	
	Bookcases	
	Bric-a-brac	
	Bureaus and Contents	
	Chairs	
	Chests and Contents	
	Closets and Contents	
	Curtains/Shades	
	Desk	
	Dresser and Contents	
	Dresser Table	
	Lamps	
	Mattresses	
	Rugs	
	Sewing Machine	
	Box Springs	
	Tables	
	Shelving	
	Mirrors	
	Wall Hangings	
	Other:	

ADDITIONAL DESCRIPTION OF ITEMS IF NECESSARY

Bedrooms

NUMBER OF ITEMS	DESCRIPTION OF ITEM	EST. VALUE ($)
	Air-conditioner Window Units	
	Bedding	
	Beds	
	Books	
	Bookcases	
	Bric-a-brac	
	Bureaus and Contents	
	Chairs	
	Chests and Contents	
	Closets and Contents	
	Curtains/Shades	
	Desk	
	Dresser and Contents	
	Dresser Table	
	Lamps	
	Mattresses	
	Rugs	
	Sewing Machine	
	Box Springs	
	Tables	
	Shelving	
	Mirrors	
	Wall Hangings	
	Other:	

ADDITIONAL DESCRIPTION OF ITEMS IF NECESSARY

Bedrooms

NUMBER OF ITEMS	DESCRIPTION OF ITEM	EST. VALUE ($)
	Air-conditioner Window Units	
	Bedding	
	Beds	
	Books	
	Bookcases	
	Bric-a-brac	
	Bureaus and Contents	
	Chairs	
	Chests and Contents	
	Closets and Contents	
	Curtains/Shades	
	Desk	
	Dresser and Contents	
	Dresser Table	
	Lamps	
	Mattresses	
	Rugs	
	Sewing Machine	
	Box Springs	
	Tables	
	Shelving	
	Mirrors	
	Wall Hangings	
	Other:	

ADDITIONAL DESCRIPTION OF ITEMS IF NECESSARY

Office/Study

NUMBER OF ITEMS	DESCRIPTION OF ITEM	EST. VALUE ($)
	Air-conditioner Wall Units	
	Books	
	Bookcases	
	Bric-a-brac	
	Cabinets and Contents	
	Card Table	
	Chairs	
	Closets and Contents	
	Couches	
	Curtains/Shades	
	Desk	
	Fireplace Equipment	
	Lamps	
	Organ	
	Piano	
	Rugs	
	Tables	
	Shelving	
	Wall Hangings	
	Plants	
	Other:	

ADDITIONAL DESCRIPTION OF ITEMS IF NECESSARY

Bathrooms

NUMBER OF ITEMS	DESCRIPTION OF ITEM	EST. VALUE ($)
	Cabinets and Contents	
	Closet Contents	
	Clothes Hamper	
	Electrical Appliances	
	Linens	
	Scales	
	Unique Equipment (shower massage, whirlpool, etc.)	

ADDITIONAL DESCRIPTION OF ITEMS IF NECESSARY

Hall

NUMBER OF ITEMS	DESCRIPTION OF ITEM	EST. VALUE ($)
	Bric-a-brac	
	Cabinets and Contents	
	Chairs	
	Closet and Contents	
	Curtains/Shades	
	Lamps	
	Rugs	
	Tables	
	Wall Hangings	
	Fixtures	
	Other:	

ADDITIONAL DESCRIPTION OF ITEMS IF NECESSARY

Den

NUMBER OF ITEMS	DESCRIPTION OF ITEM	EST. VALUE ($)
	Air-conditioner Wall Units	
	Books	
	Bookcases	
	Bric-a-brac	
	Cabinets and Contents	
	Card Table	
	Chairs	
	Closet and Contents	
	Couches	
	Curtains/Shades	
	Desk	
	Fireplace Equipment	
	Lamps	
	Organ	
	Piano	
	Rugs	
	Tables	
	Shelving	
	Wall Hangings	
	Plants	
	Other:	

ADDITIONAL DESCRIPTION OF ITEMS IF NECESSARY

Garage

NUMBER OF ITEMS	DESCRIPTION OF ITEM	EST. VALUE ($)
	Auto Repair Equipment	
	Garden Tools	
	Lawn Furniture	
	Lawn Games	
	Power Equipment	
	Portable Heaters	
	Chain Saw	
	Boat & Equipment	
	Hand Tools	
	Other:	

ADDITIONAL DESCRIPTION OF ITEMS IF NECESSARY

Basement/Workshop

NUMBER OF ITEMS	DESCRIPTION OF ITEM	EST. VALUE ($)
	Bric-a-brac	
	Chairs	
	Dehumidifier	
	Humidifier	
	Clothes Dryer	
	Hand Tools	
	Power Tools	
	Heating Unit	
	Luggage	
	Other Equipment:	
	Piano	
	Rugs	
	Tables	
	Trunk and Contents	
	Washing Machine	
	Workbench	
	Pool Table	
	Games	
	Collections	

Basement/Workshop (Cont.)

NUMBER OF ITEMS	DESCRIPTION OF ITEM	EST. VALUE ($)
	Wall Hangings	
	Bar Items (refrigerator, blender, etc.)	
	Exercise Equipment	

ADDITIONAL DESCRIPTION OF ITEMS IF NECESSARY

Attic

NUMBER OF ITEMS	DESCRIPTION OF ITEM	EST. VALUE ($)
	Furniture	
	Luggage	
	Trunks and Contents	
	Collections	
	Other Stored Items:	

ADDITIONAL DESCRIPTION OF ITEMS IF NECESSARY

Suppliers and Manufacturers

Alarm Equipment Suppliers:

Ademco-Division of
  Pittway Corp.
165 Eileen Way
Syosett, NY 11791
516-921-6700

Arrowhead Security Distribution
120 Interstate North,
  Parkway East
Atlanta, GA 30339
800-848-9999

Fire Burglary Instruments, Inc.
50 Engineers Road
Hauppauge, NY 11788
516-582-6161

FeelSafe, Inc.
  (nationwide outlets)
50 Engineers Road
Hauppauge, NY 11788
800-645-5430

Mountain West
4215 N. 16th Street
P.O. Box 10780, Dept-T
Phoenix, AZ 85064-0780
800-528-6169

Full Service Manufacturers:

ADT Security Systems
300 Interpace Parkway
Parsippany, NJ 07054
201-316-1200

Crime Control Inc.
2601-T Fortune Circle E
Indianapolis, IN 46241
317-247-7770

Sentry Protective Systems Corp.
150 Liverpool St.
East Boston, MA 02128
617-569-9700

Index